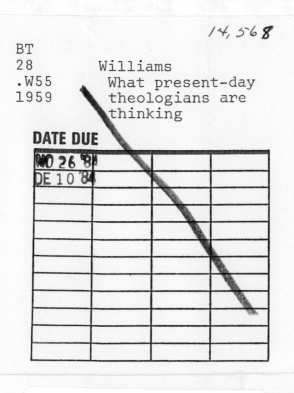

Harper ▲ ChapelBooks

WHAT PRESENT-DAY THEOLOGIANS ARE THINKING

THIRD EDITION, REVISED

Daniel Day Williams

Harper ChapelBooks
Harper & Row, Publishers
New York, Evanston, and London

CONTENTS

PREFACE
TO THE THIRD EDITION

CHRISTIAN THEOLOGIANS are carrying on a conversation today which is of the greatest importance for the Christian church and for all men who are looking for a constructive faith. Because I believe in the importance of that conversation, I have written this book to try to say briefly and in a nontechnical way what theologians are about. I have done less than justice to those who are selected for discussion. My purpose is to show that certain key problems lie at the heart of the theological movement today as it appears in many different Christian communions. I try to state what these problems are, to show what theologians are saying in the attempt to solve them, and to indicate how a significant meeting of minds is leading to helpful results today.

Theologians, I believe, ought to try to say not only to one another but to laymen what theology is about, and what we think is being accomplished. This is a different task from technical scholarship; but a necessary one if the Christian message is to be interpreted at a critical level for all who would understand it.

The present edition of this study of contemporary theology is written with awareness that the period of theological thought from the end of the first World War to the middle of the century has come to a turning point in the years 1960–66. What I have called the "theological renaissance" with its emphasis upon justification by faith, its polemic for the biblical faith against the synthesis of liberal Christianity, the dominance of such magisterial theological con-

11

structions as those of Karl Barth and Paul Tillich has now entered a new phase. There is a radical new questioning of the relationship of the church to the world, and of the task of theology in an age dominated by scientific technology.

In the light of some of the present trends, such as the questioning of the structure of traditional theological doctrines, the calling for a reconsideration of the meaning of God's action in the world, even the so-called "death of God" theologies, it is tempting to think that the theological situation should be approached as something entirely new. This would, I believe, be a great mistake. What we are seeing in this period of the 1960s is the working out and reassessment of the total movement of modern theology. We cannot understand the present questioning about God and the situationist movement in ethics without considering what has been done in the past fifty years to define the issues involved. It is important, therefore, to examine the analysis of the development of theology in the first half of the century. I have added an entire new chapter on the present discussion of God and the world, and new sections to the ethical discussions centering in the situationist or contextualist position.

Another major turn has occurred since 1960. The Second Vatican Council has thrown open the structure of Roman Catholic Faith and practice to new emphases, new positions, and a new meeting with other faiths. An adequate consideration of the theological significance of Vatican II would require an analysis extending far beyond the scope of this brief book. There are and will be, of course, innumerable resources for studying the Council's work. In the present volume I have been able only to take account of certain fundamental points where everything said before 1960 is now out of date. Also I have tried to show how the earlier work of Catholic theologians has been preparing for the reconstruction brought about by the Council. The theological discussion arising from this great event of Christian history will form a new ecumenical context for theology from this time forward.

No interpretation of the biblical faith should be made today without mention of the discovery in the caves of the Judean desert of the libraries and other remains of the Qumran community, the Dead Sea Scrolls, the discoveries of gnostic collections of sayings attributed to Jesus, and the discoveries of Ras Shamra which may throw so much light on the Old Testament background. The number of books and papers dealing with the Scrolls quickly reached the thousands. General accounts for English readers are in Millar Burrows' two books and Frank Cross' *The Ancient Library of Qumran*. A valuable collection of essays dealing with the significance of the new discoveries for Christian thought is *The Scrolls and the New Testament* edited by Krister Stendahl. Robert Grant has given a concise and valuable discussion of the gnostic materials in *The Secret Sayings of Jesus*.

While the Scrolls are of immense importance for our understanding of the rise of Christianity, they enlarge but do not fundamentally alter our knowledge of the setting of the life of Jesus and the message of the New Testament. They have sharpened our awareness that the Christian knowledge of God comes in the web of human history. It does not descend as a full-blown doctrine and liturgy out of relation to its historical preparation.

Since this book deals mainly with the internal discussion among theologians, I should like to add this brief note about the increasing attention being given to the place of Christianity as faith and religion among the religions of the world. Arnold Toynbee in his *Christianity among the Religions of the World* has spoken of the "vein of exclusiveness and intolerance in Christianity" and has declared his conviction that "all the living higher religions ought to subordinate their traditional rivalries and make a new approach toward one another in face of a fearful common adversary, a revival of the worship of collective human power, armed with new weapons, both material and spiritual" (pp. 85, 97).

Sharply different views are to be found among Christians on the many questions here raised. Well-known books on the problems are Hendrick Kraemer's *The Christian Message in a Non-Christian World*, and William Ernest Hocking's *Living Religions and a World Faith*. Each has written a new book on the topic: Kraemer's *Religion and the Christian Faith*, and Hocking's *The Coming World Civilization*. Wilfred Cantwell Smith's *The Meaning and End of Religion* is an important study by an historian of religion. H. H. Farmer's Gifford Lectures, *Revelation and Religion*, are on this topic, and Canon Raven's Gifford Lectures are closely related to it. Floyd Ross's book, *Addressed to Christians: Isolationism vs. World-Community*, seeks a positive rapprochement between Christianity and the other religions. A. C. Bouquet's *The Christian Faith and Non-Christian Religions* offers an extensive review of the present situation of Christianity in the world where there is a remarkable revival of the self-consciousness of all the great faiths. Toynbee's word about the threat of new forms of political and technological power recalls the context in which the religions confront one another today. The problem of Christianity in a world contending with new forms of power is ably reviewed in Charles West's *Communism and the Theologians: Study of an Encounter*.

This book has grown out of many theological discussions through the years, and I am grateful to all the colleagues and students who have encouraged me and contributed to my thinking. There are my colleagues in *Duodecim,* a theological discussion group. There are those who discussed the Mead-Swing Lectures at Oberlin School of Theology and the participants in the seminar in contemporary theology at the dedication of Marsh Chapel at Boston University. The responsibility for the positions taken here is, of course, my own.

I gratefully acknowledge the help of Helen and Paul Davis on the original manuscript and index. The preparation of the present manuscript has been greatly aided by the skillful cooperation of Mrs. Margot Biersdorff. My wife has not only given countless hours of expert help, but also the understanding and support which makes it possible to work at all.

D.D.W.

February 7, 1966
New York City

CHAPTER I

The Theological Renaissance

OUR AIM is to see what is going on in Christian thought today by examining the discussion of five themes: first, authority and the Bible; second, God and the World; third, the basis of Christian ethics; fourth, the meaning of Jesus Christ; and fifth, the nature of the Church. In this chapter we need to establish some common ground for understanding what it is that marks theological thinking off from other kinds of thinking, and yet keeps theology always responsive to the intellectual situation in which it exists. Theological work does not go on in a vacuum. It must respond to the spiritual and ideological issues of its time. Therefore, we need to characterize the central theme of theology and to take notice of the formative elements in the present situation which help to explain what Christian thinkers are reacting against, what resources they find in the present situation, and why they interpret the Gospel today in the way in which they do.

I

There is a theological renaissance today. It may seem strange to speak of one, for is there not theology wherever there is Christian thinking about the meaning of the faith? Indeed anyone who thinks about the meaning of life is raising the questions with which theology wrestles. What is the origin of our life? What is it all about? What is our destiny in history and beyond the boundary line of death? Serious probing of these questions is always "theological" because it involves us in giving answers to questions which cut to the roots of our whole existence. What then does it mean to

17

speak of a rebirth of theology today?

What has happened is that there is throughout Christendom a new determination to find what it is that makes Christianity a decisively different faith from all others. What is it that gives Christianity its own integrity and its independent standard of judgment over against all other philosophies and causes which bid for the allegiance of men? The rebirth of theology means a renewal of the effort to discover the foundations of the Christian life. Since Karl Barth's *Commentary on Romans*, the first edition of which was published in 1918, there has been a deepening consciousness that there is a radical settlement to be made between Christianity and the thought and values of the modern world. This settlement cannot be one of simple accommodation. In the modern period of Christianity there was an emphasis on the question, "How can the Christian faith be made intelligible within and in harmony with the highest idealism and scientific thought of our civilization?" Now the question is, "What is there in the Christian faith which gives us such an understanding of ourselves that we must assert our loyalty to the Holy God above all the splendid and yet corruptible values of our civilization?"

That there is a reality at the base of all Christian living which gives us our reason for being and the final test for all our decisions, is the conviction upon which theological work depends. This life-giving reality might be called the "substance of faith" if substance were not such a static word. It means that living truth of God's ultimately compelling word to us in Jesus Christ. Alan Richardson affirms the central fact that "there is an identity of faith which underlies all its expressions, and that this 'hard core' of faith is itself not ideological in essence."[1] Ideology is a projection of human values outward into the divine. Faith is an appreciation of the divine reality received from God for the transformation of our lives.

One obvious sign of the new spirit in theology is that such Biblical words as Creation, Redemption, Resurrection, and Last Things have come to appear as more indispensable for us than was recognized in the modern period. Of course terms such as "integration," "value creation," "social progress," can be just as "theological" as Biblical terms. That is, they can be used to express the Christian convictions about God and life. But the distinctive vocabulary of the Bible has reasserted itself for many who thought its terms could be replaced. No other words seem able to bear the freight of meaning which Sin, Reconciliation, and Atonement have. The core of the faith seems intimately bound up with the original language which expresses it.

An objection to the statement that there is a theological renaissance might be that we are talking about only that small part of the whole church which went through the modernist movement. The great orthodox traditions in Rome, of the Eastern Church, and in Protestantism have stood by the traditional dogmas through the whole modern period. But the matter is not so simple. There is a renaissance of theology in these traditions today just at the point where the inherited forms of expressing the faith have been called into question. Christian theology in its very nature continually must try to "say over again" in the light of new knowledge and reflection what the faith means. The president of an American seminary in the last century who expressed his gratitude at the close of his administration that no new idea had ever been put forth under his leadership was going counter to the whole history of the Christian church. And, of course, he was exposing the staleness of a petrified orthodoxy. Just now the orthodox traditions are themselves in ferment. New ways of stating the faith are being sought so that the very tradition itself may be alive with meaning for a restless humanity which has new problems, and new terms for asking its questions.

Where Christian theology is most alive today it expresses a double determination. It seeks to uncover that in the Christian faith which brings a new perspective into human existence beyond all the limited and circumscribed values of human culture. At the same time it tries to show that theology itself lies under the judgment of the living and personal revelation of God. It therefore moves against all simple traditionalism and orthodoxy to try to show how the meaning of the Bible, of the faith, and of the tradition itself becomes most real for us when we encounter it again with freedom and with fresh questions. Theological work is not in itself the sheer proclamation of the Gospel. It stands on the field where the Gospel meets the spirit of the times in which we stand. Its function is to enable that meeting to take place at the level of the deepest intellectual searching and the most radical questioning of the meaning of existence.

II

We shall state in this chapter some of the important formative influences in the present spiritual and intellectual situation which help to explain what contemporary theology is about. The meaning of these factors for theology can be clear only if we keep in mind what it is that the Christian faith asserts as the truth about human life; for it is in the meeting of basic Christian convictions with the faiths and philosophies of our own time that the decisive conflicts and the creative theological work can take place.

Any attempt to state the ultimate Christian convictions is certain to be inadequate. Christians have always expressed their faith in such diverse ways that one can plausibly argue there is no structural unity in the Christian view of things. There is only the unity of a historical movement which has a few shared symbols and shared memories. A well-known liberal theologian used to define Christianity as the religion of all those who have called themselves

Christian. And he apparently believed that any further characterizing definition would leave someone out. But while there are many kinds of Christianity and many doctrines, there is something more fundamental in which unity can be found. There is a fundamental character of the Christian perspective on life which can never be perfectly expressed but which gives to the faith its continuing power to create a community of understanding. It is possible to be so impressed with theological diversity that we forget all the diversity would be meaningless unless behind it there is a controlling and directing substance of faith which has an enduring integrity. We can express this integrating perspective of the Christian faith in three affirmations.

The first article of Christian faith is that man has one and only one true object of worship. There is one Holy God, creator of heaven and earth. He is Lord of all life. To him we are beholden for our life in all its meaning and all its hope. Monotheism for the Christian means that anything else which is put in the place of our loyalty to God is an idol. The worship of national power, or racial prestige, or financial success, or cultural tradition is a violation of the one truth about our life, that all created things come from God. To commit life to the one true God is to refuse to have any other gods at all. Values there are in abundance, interests, plans, programs, loyalties to family and nation. But these are not gods. They do not save us. They are not holy in themselves.

The second assertion in the Christian faith concerns its two-sided estimate of human nature. Man is made for God. Man can despoil his holy destiny. When the Christian asks who God is he answers that we have God's revelation in a human life. The Christian faith says that God has in his fullness manifested himself in the coming of Jesus of Nazareth, his life, his deeds, his teachings, his announcement of the Kingdom of God, his death on the cross, the conviction of his disciples that death did not hold his life, but that the reality they knew in Jesus was present, risen, among them. This story of Jesus' life and death, seen from the standpoint of Christian faith, discloses both the high dignity of man as bearer of the image of God and the final problem of man as one capable of using his freedom against the loving purpose of God.

The positive estimate of man in Christianity stems from the belief that man in his freedom, in his creative power, in his personal worth, is the bearer of the high good at which the whole creation aims. Man is a creature; but he is that creature who is conscious of his own dependence. He can stand in personal confrontation with the Lord of his existence. He can commit his life to the doing of God's holy will. Therefore Christianity always ultimately finds itself ranged on the side of a true humanism. Any creative expression of the essential spirit of man, any use of human powers to develop, extend and enhance the full powers of human life is a positive good for the Christian faith. Human existence is disfigured by machines which dull the sense of worth, by the exploitation of the mind in propagandistic lying, and by the political destruction of freedom. The Christian demand is: Release the human powers. Heal human sickness. Build the decent society. God has used the human as the image of his own being. In Jesus Christ he has taken up human life into his own will and sanctified all of it, even its longing, its suffering, and its dying, for all these he made the means of expressing his love.

The Christian call for the release of human powers has one supreme restriction. This release must always be under the constraint of the service of the reality which is not man's own good alone, but which is God's own holy will. For man is his own worst enemy. The greatest threat to the realization of human good comes from within man himself. It does not come primarily from some "bad" men who can be neatly distinguished from the rest.

It comes from all. For man in his freedom can set something less than God's holy will in the center of life and give his allegiance to that. Sin is man's creation of a false God, and a flight from the true God. Its consequence is the tearing of the holy fabric of life. It is a plunge into the abyss where the human spirit feeds only upon itself and destroys itself.

We cannot understand the depth of the Christian doctrine of sin if we give to it only a moral connotation. To break the basic laws of justice and decency is sin indeed. Man's freedom to honor principles is the moral dimension in his nature, and sin often appears as lawlessness. But sin has its roots in something which is more than the will to break the law. The core of sin is our making ourselves the center of life, rather than accepting the holy God as the center. Lack of trust, self-love, pride, these are three ways in which Christians have expressed the real meaning of sin. The consequence of sin is in the self-imposed loneliness of a loveless life. There is a mystery of evil in life over and above sin. But what sin does is to make the struggle with evil meaningless. When we refuse to hold our freedom in trust and reverence for God's will, there is nothing which can make the risk of life worth the pain of it.

The third Christian affirmation is that God makes possible a new life for sinful men. We are not doomed forever to walk on this knife-edge of eternity with the threat of utter loss on one side and some tentative human good on the other. God in his own way has enabled man to walk with faith, with love, and with hope. The way to the new life is forgiveness. This means that the same God who has given us this life, and who stands in judgment over our sin, accepts us as we are, offering us a new life within his love. The way through must begin with this act of God toward us, for we cannot do it for ourselves. When we know with our whole being that the door is open to the sinner to return to the way of love, there is a release from fear and from the self-destructive plunge into idolatry.

The meaning of the new life is personal existence in faith, in humility, and in love. It is life in faith for its center is not ourselves but the God who has shown himself both our Lord and our Redeemer. It is life in humility for we have it only through God's forgiveness toward us. All that we have and are, all the good that we may under God achieve, is ours only because God uses our broken efforts to work out his holy cause. It is life in love, for love means to the Christian sacrificial self-giving for the community of all and the continuing forgiveness which creates a new community of life out of estranged and broken existence. The love which we are to give to one another is not primarily a perfect ethical attitude. It is the spirit of those who have been bound together in a new way deeper than morality because only through God's sacrificial act have they been able to come together at all. In William Temple's fine words, "For the Christian, every man is the brother for whom Christ died." Those who live by this faith are bound into a community of the faithful. To be "in Christ" is to live as one of his "congregation." It is to live in his Church. This is the real meaning of "church," not merely a social institution, though it is that, and not only an intimate spiritual fellowship of a few, but a new people in human history, who have become a new people because God has shown mercy. He has created a new order of life in this restored community between himself and man. The Church is the company of those who have a new life because this has happened to them.

When we say that Christian faith leads to a new community between God and his people we make the decisive affirmation of the Gospel against the deepest sickness of the human spirit. There is a desperate search for community today. Any Christian analysis of man's plight will point directly to the breakdown of the ties which make us belong in a human way to one another. Our desperation when we cannot find genuine mutual relationships with others betrays itself in the way that we seek to create loyalty by force or technique. Racial groups, national groups, seek to impose narrow and restricted community upon us. Anyone who offers us a group which is asserting itself makes us feel taller and stronger. This is what the "titanism" in modern paganism means. The Christian faith opposes all community based on false superiority and destruction of others. In an essay which exposes the frantic destructiveness of modern "titanism" with its counterpart in the doctrine that "Hell is our neighbor," Norberto Bobbio states the real theme of the Christian understanding of man: "The value of man cannot be dissociated from his state as a social being, in the sense that man, as a necessarily co-existent being, is significant not *per se,* as being the manifestation of an absolute substance, but in respect of what he gives or can give to the society of which he forms part, in so far as he actually cooperates, or is afforded an opportunity to cooperate with others."[2]

The universal theme of the theological renaissance today is that the true human community can come into existence, not through human effort alone, but through a discovery that God through his own forgiving love does bring men into a sane, humble and personally creative relationship. It has never been easy to make the meaning of this Christian claim clear or convincing. The truth of the Christian faith can never be possessed once for all. That would destroy the reality of our life in personal freedom. Life in the truth of God is always a life being reborn. What we may hope for today is that in our need to find a sane and tolerable basis for life together, we will discover the way to a fresh hearing of the Gospel word as to where the ultimate source of a genuine human community is to be found. At the intellectual level this means that theology must engage in a continuing conversation with the profoundest expressions of contemporary human experience, regardless of whether or not they appear in secular form. It must be especially attentive when searching questions about traditional Christian beliefs are raised. We must now examine some areas of thought today where theology finds specific challenges to Christian beliefs, and where there are resources for the creative interpretation of the abiding Gospel.

III

When the political community turns itself into a religious rival for the loyalty of men, Christianity faces a new form of an ancient enemy. That is what has happened. Whoever would understand Christian theology today must see it against the background of the issue which is joined between the Christian loyalty to the God who is creator and judge of all nations, and the totalitarian claims over the souls of men which the Nazis and Fascists and the Russian Communists make. Out of the struggles of nations in the world-wide revolution new idols have been created in the form of particular powers and leaders whose word is absolute law. These are known to be idols from the Christian standpoint because they set one group of mankind in a place of peculiar moral favor. They give a human elite absolute power over the minds and lives of other human beings. They usurp God's prerogatives.

Inevitably the new idolatries seek to destroy every kind of loyalty, religious, scientific or humanistic, which sets any truth above the control of men. It was in the fight of the German confessional church group against the Nazis that this conflict came to its most decisive engagement so far in modern times. It would be difficult to exaggerate the importance of this struggle against the Hitler regime for the present theological situation. Here it was made plain that the Church must publicly assert its primary loyalty to the God it knows in Jesus Christ, or cease to be the

Christian Church. The Church is driven back to the very fundamentals of faith. What is the rock upon which faith in God stands, no matter what waves of violence and torture may beat against it?

This struggle gave warning that much of what may appear to be vitality in a nation, or even in the Christian Church, may be captured and perverted by a soul-destroying idolatry. The Nazis exploited the new sense of community and common purpose which came with a reassertion of national power. There were many German Christians who thought some kind of compromise could be made with National Socialism, or who even regarded it as a spiritual movement which Christianity could bless and direct. But the historical development showed that a national spirit which claims exclusive allegiance cannot tolerate the Christian doctrine of God as Lord and judge over all peoples. The problem is to make plain and invincible that Christian criterion of judgment which puts the God of the Christian faith first. One who participated in this struggle, Dr. Paul Tillich, has stated what this issue means theologically by using a Greek word *"diastasis"* which means "cutting." The Church must achieve a *diastasis* which sets it free from "entangling alliances" with idolatrous loyalties.[3] Tillich goes on to say that in the German situation it was the confessional theology, with Karl Barth as its leader, which alone was able to cut the faith free and create an effective center of spiritual resistance.

The key to the confessional groups' resistance was expressed in the Barmen declaration. This asserted that Christian faith rests upon the word of God in Jesus Christ, as that word is testified to in the Bible, and it rests on nothing else. When Christ stands before Pilate the word of God is there in the One Man. It is not to be found in any normative way in the state or in the representative of the state who in a worldly sense pronounces a legal sentence of death upon the Christ.

The German crisis showed that the Bible in spite of its pre-scientific world view can be shown to point unequivocally to the Holy God through its essential content, Jesus Christ. It also seems to be true that modern scientific and philosophical systems may lack the power to offer such an effective opposition. The Bible cannot be treated merely as a relic of past beliefs and outgrown religious thinking. The truth which it proclaims has become the last line of defense against modern lies and inhumanity.

This new revelation of the power and authority of the Biblical message lies back of much that is happening in theology today. Yet it must be seen that to assert the authority of the Bible gives no simple solution of the problem of Christian truth. It puts the old problem of faith and reason in a new intellectual setting. Two considerations make this plain. In the first place, while it may be truly said that the confessional Christians were the only organized group resistance to the Nazi movement, there was opposition from other sources. The whole tradition of Western humanism which has its origin partly in Jewish Christian faith, but also in Greek thought, and which has had one of its supreme expressions in the enlightenment in Germany, sets many human values against the inhumanity of totalitarianism. There were those who resisted the Nazi movement to the death on grounds of humanitarian idealism, and a humanistic faith in rational justice.

The Christian faith has an important ally in the humanistic ideals of our civilization. This ally ought not to be cast aside. The Biblical message must be shown to accept and to fulfill the human quests for truth and justice. It is often said by Christian apologists that Western humanitarian ideals are drawn from Christian sources. In large part this is true. Even so this does not allow us to forget that traditions of justice and freedom in human relations have come to have their own independent life and allegiance in our culture. It will not do simply to reject the positive worth of those elements because they have been separated from Christian rootage.

A second consideration reinforces this first. It is not enough to defy the false gods. There must be positive guidance for the creation of a just society. To do the first does not in itself lead directly to a solution of the second. While the Biblical message is the center of the Christian's political and cultural outlook, we must relate it to a positive appreciation of the values and ideals which help to create human communities of law, of art, of science, and of creative community life.

We have the question then of how the problem of political idols is to be viewed in the nations where elements of a free and just society do exist. The necessary starting point is the acknowledgment that no nation is free of temptations to idolatry. It is possible to identify a particular economic system or "the values of Western civilization" with the will of God, forgetting on the one hand how precarious some of the gains toward freedom and democracy are when threatened by the hysterical repression of thought or the struggle for racial equality; and on the other hand, how varied and uncertain are the particular forms which a free society must take in the light of historical factors in each situation. Compare the problem of establishing political justice in the New England town of the seventeenth century, in a modern metropolis of eight million, in a nation of 150 million, and in the new states of Ghana and Indonesia. The ultimate values of human life and dignity are the same, but how varied and complex is the task of conserving them. An editorial writer for *Life* magazine asked the question in this form: "What then is the true relation between the cause of Christianity and the cause of Western civilization? Americans are now in the presence of that question. Perhaps its answer is this: there is a relation, but those who make it an identity fall into the cardinal Christian sin of pride."[4] Even this wise comment would seem somewhat parochial to Asians who view "Western civilization" with a more critical eye.

The problem of the authority of the Bible and its message, which we shall examine in the next chapter, is, we see, no abstract problem. How can the Biblical message lead to a Christian critique of all human ideals and philosophies, and at the same time support a positive appreciation of the truth which comes through science, philosophy, and the give and take of human experience? A sound theological answer to this question becomes a matter of life and death for a free society.

IV

Christian theology in any age works within a "climate of thought." The currents of thought in a given time make up a large part of theologians' intellectual equipment. The intellectual life in a culture offers both resources and problems in the interpretation of the faith. In one sense the Christian Gospel never has a really favorable intellectual climate. This is partly because human culture always produces a measure of skepticism about all religious belief. Some of it takes the form of dogmatic atheism, some plain indifference, and there are the humanistic and positivistic philosophies which seek the good life without God. More than this there is the fact that all satisfaction in human intellectual achievements, as if the good as we discern it is the true good, is called into question in the shattering reality of the cross. Here the best as well as the worst of human life is judged and found wanting. Even the religiously good could not tolerate the humble love of God. The scandal of the cross to man's self-confident assurance remains a scandal.

Yet every Christian theology, and the Bible itself, shows that the Christian mind depends on a continuing interaction with the human quests. It has a triple relation to the thought of a culture.

It tries to preserve the integrity of the faith against whatever would destroy it. It becomes "apologetics" when it seeks to find some common understanding with those who do not yet believe, in order to open the way for faith. Finally, it appropriates the insight and critical tools which science, philosophy and art may provide. A simple illustration is offered by logic. All theology depends upon the logical structure of language, and the critical tool of analysis which logical theory provides. Yet logic is not a product of faith in any direct sense, but of reflective thought about experience. The same principle applies to the most important aspects of Christian faith. Paul, for example, finds in the Gospel a truth which goes far beyond the insight of the Greek mystery religions. But Paul's form of expression and to some extent the very structure of his religious experience takes something from the Hellenistic mystery cults. He saw that to be "in Christ" is the Christian answer to the quest of the mystery religions for participation in the life of God who conquers death. The language of faith uses the language of culture even when it must transmute the meaning of that language.

The dialogue between theology and contemporary culture is as complex as the culture itself, and as the shifts in theological perspective make it. The Christian faith should, as Reinhold Niebuhr has often pointed out, offer a perspective which is not captured by extravagant optimism nor by hopelessness in the face of man's situation. Modern culture offers examples of both extremes. Further, there are sober and reasoned forms of confident optimism just as there are stoic humanisms which cling to man's dignity and freedom in the face of the threat of meaninglessness. In the first group are humanists like Julian Huxley in his *Religion Without Revelation* and Charles Frankel who states *The Case for Modern Man*. In the second group are such writers as Albert Camus, Samuel Becket, and James Baldwin who are carefully listened to and with gratitude by theologians not only because of their powerful portrayal of the boundary situations and agonies of human life, but because of their stature as moral prophets, hurling themselves through their art against the stupidities and injustices of society. The Nobel prize addresses of Albert Camus and William Faulkner are notable expressions of the artists' responsibility and courage.

Theology draws insight and the possibility of communication from the artists and poets of whatever religious persuasion or of none. Amos Wilder's studies such as his *Modern Poetry and the Christian Tradition,* and Arthur McGill's *The Celebration of Flesh* are noteworthy examples of the theologically sensitive analysis of the meaning of modern poetry. Mrs. Kathleen Baxter in England, and Tom Driver, Nathan Scott, Jr., and many others have given theological analyses of modern literature. Nathan Scott's editorship of *The Tragic Vision and the Christian Faith* is a representative example of this aspect of the theological dialogue with culture. The period after mid-century is one of varied voices and clashing spirits, and theology must listen, both for the voices of men, and the word of God.

As we look now at three areas of contemporary thought, the interpretation of history, psychology and philosophy, we can document the fact that there is a new concern about the meaning of Christian faith. We can also see that theology will find critical issues posed as it relates itself to the thought of our complex culture.

The way history is viewed and written is always important for Christian thought because the Christian faith concerns the meaning of history. It can be argued the historical consciousness of Western civilization is itself a product of the Jewish Christian heritage. It was in the prophetic outlook of the Bible that *time* first became clearly viewed as the field of purposeful activity. This overcame the Greek view which tended to regard existence in time as only the passing image of the pure and unchanging realm of being.

It might appear that Christian thought would be congenial to the idea that the facts of history lead to some definite generalizations about its over-all meaning. Faith holds that God works through human history for the goal of man's redemption. Theologians and historians divide, however, over the question of what the facts of history may show. Some accept the positivist thesis that scientific historians can only record the facts. The meaning of those facts escapes science altogether. This attitude toward historical generalization has strongly influenced much historical writing since the late nineteenth century. It represents in part a reaction against the idealistic generalizations in which Hegelians and the philosophers of progress too freely indulged.

A Christian interpreter, Karl Löwith, in his *Meaning in History,* argues that our judgment on the meaning of history must come entirely from faith. If we are to live with hope we must find a meaning, but "it is the very absence of meaning in the events themselves that motivates the quest. . . . To ask earnestly the question of the ultimate meaning of history takes one's breath away; it transports us into a vacuum which only hope and faith can fill."[5] Löwith argues that our Western civilization derives its belief in the significance of history from the Christian faith that God, the creator, fulfills his purpose in the "end of all things." This eschatological faith can be believed, but the course of events in itself furnishes no evidence for its truth. We can say only that the facts cannot disprove the faith.

There are other historians, both secular and Christian, who believe that the question cannot be settled with so sharp a distinction between facts and faith as Löwith makes. Arnold Toynbee and Herbert Butterfield see some patterns of meaning in history; yet both of them reject any simple "progressive" view of history's course. And they both agree that our evaluation of the meaning of history involves a decision of faith which does go beyond the sheer weight of the observable evidence.

In his monumental *A Study of History* Toynbee tries to **derive** some of the universal patterns in the life of civilizations. There is the pattern of creative vitality responding to new challenges. There is the rise of a creative minority with its tendency to become a complacent oligarchy. There is the pattern of decay when the vital power of a civilization lapses, and men seek ways to escape the difficult call for renewal. Toynbee rejects any Spenglerian fatalism. Renewal is possible if civilizations rise to new challenges; but the way of renewal offers no simple path of progressive development. It begins in the realm of the spirit when men discover the true image of the saviour of mankind who through his own life expresses the courage of an undying hope for the world. In his more recent writings Toynbee has stressed the theme that out of the decay of civilizations with their narrow loyalties there emerges a community with universal loyalty in the form of the Church. Critics of Toynbee point out that he fails to recognize how such a community, with its universal spirit, can itself also become subject to corruption. But this criticism does not invalidate the main point that there may be some objective confirmation of the Christian interpretation of history through tracing patterns of development, crisis and renewal.[6] In his *Faith and History* Reinhold Niebuhr has strongly argued that faith must find some partial confirmation in its illumination of historical happenings.

The British historian, Herbert Butterfield, in his engaging *Christianity and History,* stands somewhere between Toynbee and Löwith. He agrees with both that there is a faith-judgment involved in recognizing any divine presence in history. "I am unable to see how a man can find the hand of God in secular history, unless he has first found that he has an assurance of it in his personal experience."[7] Butterfield is skeptical about attempts to fit history into patterns of "cycles" or "spirals" or other analogies. History is not so neat. One analogy alone he thinks may be reasonably adequate. To live in history is like playing an orchestral score which the players are seeing for the first time. Further, the composer is still at work giving us a few new bars at a time. At the same time Butterfield points out that the Christian faith, with its central attention upon the life of Jesus, is concerned about the objective historical facts. He also believes that there are some universal structures in history to which theology supplies many clues. One important idea is the universal sinfulness of men. Without that presupposition the historian cannot rightly understand the history he is looking at because he will miss the effect of the presumption of men and nations which leads them to overreach themselves and destroy their own causes. There is, then, a discernible form of judgment in history. There is the weaving together of many conditions and consequences into processes which we can neither impose nor alter. And in some ways which we do not plan, good rises again out of shattering evil.

As Butterfield points out, there is an eagerness today to see human destiny in some frame of meaning which is akin to what the Old Testament prophets proclaimed. They tried to discern the enduring moral order as it is reflected in the tangled web of events. The very conception that man's life is a history of freedom and fate moving in relation to the creative and holy will of God is an idea where theologians and historians can have a mutually fruitful discussion. They do not need to fall into the barren warfare of pious dogma against objective science. Christian dogma must illuminate the facts, and science needs the interpretation of faith.

If contemporary historians tend to stress the bewilderment of man, contemporary psychology appears frequently to offer a new religion for the soul. The patient on the psychiatrist's couch has become a widely recognized symbol of the soul's healing, supplanting for many the figure of the penitent on his knees. Our new psychological understanding of man raises some of the most fundamental questions for Christian faith.

At least at two points the movement which may be generally called "psychotherapy" has shifted from an original hostility toward religion to a more appreciative attitude toward it. The first point is the nature of the "self." Behavioristic psychology and the early Freudianism tended to look at man as a system of psycho-physical stresses and strains without any free and responsible center of integrity. But this quasi-mechanical theory proved itself incapable of interpreting the actual data with which the clinical psychologist deals. He cannot help the person without recognizing that there is a directing, organizing factor in the human make-up which seeks to preserve its own identity and to realize its own freedom. That factor is the "soul" or "self" and it is there whether or not we discard all the traditional supernatural connotations of those terms. The late Harry Stack Sullivan came to define psychology as the "science of interpersonal relations." This definition not only emphasizes the uniqueness of the personal, but it broadens the psychological field to the point where the religious approach to man must come actively into the conversation.

The second development is the way in which the analysis of mental illness has produced psychological theories which throw light upon what the profounder Christian analysis of sin has always recognized. Both theology and psychology are cutting far beneath a purely moralistic interpretation of sin. Psychologists look for the source of much mental illness in the wrong turn which the self takes in its protection against basic anxieties. The self builds a rigid wall around its own native sensitivities in order to avoid the threats which its personal and impersonal environment bring against it. It develops patterns of exploitation and dominance, or submission and escape. Instead of becoming a free self in control of his own life, it creates a "second" self which is so preoccupied with its own avoidance of hurt that it lives under a threat and a law which takes over and makes the person into something he actually does not will to be. In the New Testament Paul calls this state "bondage under the law." The released self with its psychological health of "productive love," to use Erich Fromm's term, is discovering what Paul speaks of as the freedom of the Gospel. We accept ourselves as we really are, and life as we really feel and know it. In the Christian account this self acceptance is made possible by God's coming to us in our state of bondage with his word of acceptance of us. "If God be for us, who can be against us."

It ought not to be suggested that there is a simple harmony of outlook between the new psychology and Christian faith. The studies of two theologians, Robert Bonthius in his *Christian Paths to Self-Acceptance,* and David Roberts in *Psychotherapy and a Christian View of Man,* are rightly cautious about the possibility of mutual understanding. Psychology and theology look at man from two different "angles of vision." For theology the basic relationship of life is that between man and his creator. Psychology looks at man "by himself" in the structures and feelings of his own experience. Yet the two understandings do not exclude each other. They must overlap. For man is a whole, and his relationship to God enters into every aspect of his life.

It was the Danish religious thinker, Søren Kierkegaard, who in the last century gave one of the profoundest analyses of the soul-sickness of anxious and guilt-ridden man. Kierkegaard is one of the major influences on Christian theology today. His analysis of anxiety is still classic, as Rollo May shows in his recent work on *Anxiety.* Mention of Kierkegaard leads us from psychology to philosophy for his thought is the most important single source of the modern philosophy of "existentialism" which looks upon man's existence as a finite, dying creature as the central clue to an interpretation of the world. The power of existentialism is that it expresses in philosophical terms man's loneliness, his ultimate fears, his sense that time does not bring progress, his uncertainty about eternal realities. For existentialism man's freedom is the source both of his humanity and of his despair. He must find the courage to take his existence into his own hands and dare to live his life out in a world which threatens him on every side.

Kierkegaard's existentialism was Christian. Man's problem is his relationship to God, and his salvation is God's forgiveness. In contrast, much of modern existentialism, like that of **Sartre,** is atheistic. As has been said for this philosophy, instead of God's creating the world out of nothing, man must create the world out of nothing. In Martin Heidegger's philosophy the question about God appears to be left open. The starting point is still man in his finitude, hurled into a situation he did not choose, faced with the threat of "nonbeing," and needing desperately to find the courage to assert his own freedom in authentic human existence.[8]

An existentialism without God is always close to despair. Man defies his fate only to submit to it. Such existentialism, of course, denies the Christian faith. But again we see how theology must adopt both a critical and appreciative attitude toward sensitive secular thought. Existentialism's analysis of man's problem, drawn as it is in part from Kierkegaard, stands very close to the deepest themes in the Biblical account of man. Some Christian theologians, as we shall see, rely heavily upon existentialism in so far as a philosophy can describe the human situation to which the Gospel must be addressed.

The philosophy of logical positivism in some ways is the polar opposite of existentialism, for positivism has a scientific interest in objectivity and strict verifiability as the foundations of all knowledge. Yet like existentialism, modern logical positivism has often been associated with an agnostic attitude toward belief in God. If only statements about matters of fact or abstract mathematical principles have meaning, as some positivists have held, then not only theology, but all metaphysical statements, and even all moral beliefs are illusions or at most become simply expressions of human feeling. Bertrand Russell, whose position is very close to, though not quite identified with, extreme positivism remarks:

> There remains however a vast field, traditionally included in philosophy, where scientific methods are inadequate. This field includes ultimate questions of value; science alone for example cannot prove that it is bad to enjoy the infliction of cruelty. Whatever can be known can be known by means of science; but things which are legitimately matters of feeling lie outside its province.[9]

Since Professor A. J. Ayer's *Language, Truth and Logic* was first published in 1936 with its statement of the logical positivist standpoint, a surprising new turn in the discussion has developed. We must consider it here for it appears to open up some important possibilities in the philosophical discussion of religious questions. Professor Ayer himself, along with many others, came to have doubts about the assertion that only empirical verifiability can give meaning to a statement. For example, when the positivist philosopher says all statements about what is right or wrong are purely "emotive" he is surely saying something meaningful, but what empirical experience could verify the statement?

The question raised here may be put in this way: What are the criteria for the valid use of language? There is some distinction between talking sense and nonsense. Can that distinction be given a general logical foundation? The discussion of this problem has led to the movement known as "philosophical analysis" and its results have been hailed by some as nothing less than a revolution in philosophy.[10] Some philosophers now hold that the analysis of the meaningfulness of language is the sole business of philosophy. Others regard this as but one aspect of the problem, and regret that many of the traditional questions of metaphysics and moral philosophy seem pushed aside.

Whatever side one takes, the new movement has created a considerable excitement, not least in the realm of its application to religious beliefs and ethical propositions. Much of the discussion has centered in British universities; but it is now a pervasive influence in the philosophical scene.

Undoubtedly the mood of the analytic philosophers is "ascetic" so far as religious questions are concerned. They continue the positivist concern for clarity and precision of language and for empirical testing. At the same time any theological thought that does not face the problem of the meaningfulness of its discourse fails at the point of relating faith to culture. Theologians are recognizing that the new concepts and methods in interpreting language must be understood in their relevance to theology, and must welcome the insistence on rigorous use of terms. John Hick's *Faith and Reason*, Willem Zuurdeeg's *An Analytical Philosophy of Religion*, Ian Ramsey's *Religious Language* and *Prospect for Metaphysics* under his editorship apply the analytic method to the problems of religious knowledge. *New Essays in Philosophical Theology*, edited by Antony Flew and Alasdaire MacIntyre, provides a significant discussion between theologians and philosophers.

One issue that has been raised for theology will illustrate the kind of question that has come to the fore. In theology we speak about God. We say that he creates, that he is good, that he saves the world. Now if these statements have meaning beyond being mere expressions of feeling, then there must be some way in which their truth can be established. We may put it another way around. If these statements have meaning, then they must make such a difference to our understanding of the world that certain kinds of things that could conceivably happen will not happen. For example, if we say that God is good, we must mean that something which denies or refutes that goodness will not take place.

Now let us ask, do we in fact allow our theological statements to lead us to conclusions which could conceivably be "falsified"? When something happens that appears to contradict the goodness of God, has not theology traditionally appealed to the mystery of the ways of providence? Is what we say about God compatible with everything that possibly can happen? If so, what meaning can our statements have? This question raised sharply by Anthony Flew and others has brought about a vigorous discussion between philosophers and theologians. How can theology answer the charge that statements about God cannot "function as statements because there is no possible or even conceivable method of testing their truth"?[11]

Some of the analytic philosophers believe that the meaningfulness of religious assertions can be maintained. In a now famous parable, John Wisdom imagines two people coming upon a garden which shows some signs of being tended and yet has wild growth. They debate whether a gardener comes to tend the garden. Although the question is empirically unresolvable (when we think of God as the gardener), it is still meaningful to believe that such a one is responsible for what we observe.[12] R. M. Hare appears to hold a similar view in his doctrine that religion constitutes a way of seeing the world, a *Blick*.[13] John Hick resorts to a more radical expedient to meet the empirical philosophers on their own ground when he holds that the Christian can expect the vision of God in the future life as a specific experience implied by Christian belief. The prediction of such a future occurrence can be held to meet the criterion of meaning proposed by the analysts.[14]

It appears that a new way of stating the issue of the status of religious belief in relation to human knowledge may be opened up in this discussion. But there is one consequence of the analytic philosophy which is not so often pointed out. It is that the questions which used to be debated under the heading of "natural theology" are being restated.

"Natural theology" has meant in the Christian tradition the enterprise of seeking that knowledge of God which is available through reflection upon the data of experience. In principle it is that knowledge of God which is open to everyone. The traditional "proofs of the existence of God" have been an important part of "natural theology" in the modern period. In this sense natural theology has had increasing strictures placed against it. Not all have surrendered it. Witness William Temple's *Nature, Man and God* and the work of the empirical theologians. But doubt about the validity of traditional proofs, and about the whole project of seeking knowledge of God from the order and activity of nature, has characterized much recent theology.

It is possible that the new discussion opens up the problem of natural theology over again. In speaking about God as creator and redeemer, we are certainly saying something about this world and course of events. We use words like person, Father, power, and wrath, to speak of God. Are we not, therefore, committed to making some explanation of what these words signify when used to express God's being?

A volume by a group of Anglican philosophers and theologians entitled *Faith and Logic* discusses this matter, and appears to justify the view that the doctrine of analogy of being has now reappeared in a new setting. Austin Farrer speaks of assertions about God as "parables."[15] This requires the analysis of the relation between a parable and the reality which it expresses. It is true that in this volume the theologians stress God's transcendence; but is not the question of immanence raised again? It was the doctrine of the divine immanence which led the empirical theologians to attempt to state how experience leads to insight into the nature of God. How can anything in experience be a parable for the divine unless the divine is somehow present in that experience? It would appear that the questions raised by the empirical theologians, and the tradition of natural theology, might now be re-examined in the setting of modern analytic philosophy.

One other development in philosophy today opens a new door to man's understanding of the issues of life. This is the new attention being given to the function of "myth" in enabling the mind to get at the truth. Some positivists have contributed to this analysis, though it is usually critics of positivism who find truth value in myth. The first question is whether the term "myth" must be restricted by us to the meaning of primitive tales about the gods which we can no longer believe; or whether there is a wider meaning of "myth" which points to a way of expressing meanings which is different from literal discourse but which is an essential way to express religious truth. Myth in this wider sense and poetry are very much akin; and "mytho-poetic" symbols seem to have a special relationship to the language of religion.

The importance of myth for Christian theology is instantly recognized when we recall that the Bible is filled with expressive symbols which are different from merely literal statements. There are the "primitive" myths in the Bible, such as the story of the Tower of Babel and the marriage of gods with human beings, or the appearances of angels in the New Testament accounts. But much more significant are those central formative concepts in the Bible beginning with Creation, and including the Election of Israel, the coming of the Christ, his miracles, and his resurrection from the dead, down to the assertions about final resurrection and judgment for the world. Are we dealing here with plain "matters of fact," or rather do we not have images and symbols which express Christian convictions but which escape purely rational and factual analysis?

From Plato to the present there have been both philosophers and theologians who have held that "myth" is one of the ways in which truth about ultimate matters can be expressed. Two philosophers who have recently given attention to the problem are Ernst Cassirer and Susanne Langer. For Cassirer myth is one of the two forms in which the mind unfolds its own structures of meaning, and it bears a special relation to religion in which concrete personal symbols are fundamental.[16] For Miss Langer, myth is the envisagement of the pattern of life of a particular people. Mythical thinking functions as a necessary preparation for the refined critical analysis of metaphysics. But the process is never complete. Men must return to the germinative mythical notions which give spirit and life to rational thought. "Apprehension outruns comprehension."[17]

Myths can express the destructive and idolatrous passions of men as well as their sense of the holy. This has been demonstrated in the creation by the Nazis of the "Myth of the Twentieth Century" with its irrational glorification of a synthetic "race" and a history fabricated to exploit the loyalties of a nation. The creation of semireligious saviours out of revolutionary leaders like Lenin and Stalin can be a political weapon of enormous power. Myths can exploit the irrational drives which have nothing to do with the disciplined intellectual quest for truth about God. But this does not mean we can do without this mode of symbolizing our values. Democracy has its myths: "the common man," "the American Way," the doctrine that "all men are created equal." These are hardly ideas which can be given strict scientific definition. They are rather symbolic assertions of the character of certain loyalties and faiths.

To those who believe that all the truth there is can be put into rational systems, Christian theology, with its Biblical modes of describing God's dealings with men, will appear hopelessly bound to the primitive ideas of a past age. But today when men are more sensitive to the need for ways of expressing the meaning of life which reach beyond the literal forms of discourse, the way may be prepared for a deeper receptiveness to the Biblical conceptions. Poetry and myth are not to be opposed to reason. They are forms of a more personal and concrete apprehension of truth than the plodding explications of reason can satisfactorily achieve.

Myth is in some ways closer to art than to philosophy. One of the ways in which Christian faith remains a fructifying force in our culture is through the creative language of art. Art which is not specifically Christian but which communicates man's sense of the holy or his hunger and thirst for it prepares the spirit for faith. Christian art typified by the poetry of Milton or Auden, the *B Minor Mass* of Bach, or the modern settings of the Mass by Poulenc or Stravinski, the novels of Dostoevski or a novel such as Alan Paton's *Cry, the Beloved Country,* the painting which keeps the story of the Christ alive in countless ways, is a means by which the basic ideas that theology criticizes and analyzes are given powerful expression. Theology is in its analytical and critical work closer to philosophy than it is to art. But theology keeps a more constant relation to mythical and poetic forms of expression than does most philosophy. Art and liturgy are the dramatic emotion-laden ways in which the message which theology interprets finds a universal language in each generation.

In sum, theology finds both new problems and new resources in the present intellectual situation which displays the breaking up of the self-confident rationalistic optimism that presented itself as an alternative to Christian faith in the modern period. Theology never depends primarily upon the base provided by cultural insight into religious values. It has its own witness to the truth revealed in Jesus Christ. Science and philosophy point toward that truth; and in the end, Christian truth must form one unbroken fabric with all truth, for Christ is the Logos incarnate. But as long as our human thinking represents a construct out of our own limited experience, involving our own self-centered perspectives, the word of God addressed to us will call into question the adequacy and finality of our formulas. Christian faith holds to a criterion which judges cultural and theological idols. At the same time, it accepts the wisdom and honesty resident in man's life, because our humanity reflects the image of God. Unless theology could enter into a continual conversation with all men on the basis of human wisdom and experience, it would remain esoteric and irrelevant.

V

Theology is revitalized not only by its discussion with thought outside the church, but also by the discussion among the diverse traditions within the church. The Vatican Council has brought about a re-statement of Roman Catholic doctrine on fundamental matters and has opened the way to a far reaching dialogue with other Christians and contemporary culture. Not since the Protestant Reformation has there been so widespread a movement for the radical re-examination of theological traditions as there is at the present time.

The ecumenical movement is largely responsible for the present world-wide communication between different Christian viewpoints. The World Council of Churches is continuing the work of the great ecumenical conferences with its study programs to which theologians of all participating churches contribute.

What must not be overlooked in the emphasis on ecumenical studies is the extent to which important developments are taking place within the various Christian communions. In the United States, for example, one prominent feature of the theological picture is the breaking up of the rigid traditionalism of many denominational groups. This can be seen in the various Lutheran bodies where the inertia of traditional orthodoxy gives many signs of having spent its force, and where a fresh theological encounter with the Biblical message is taking place. The same can be said about groups such as the Congregationalists, who have been as thoroughly entrenched in a fixated liberalism as their conservative brethren are in their traditions. In the Congregational churches there is a general deepening of the liberalism through an emphasis on the themes of sin and grace in the evangelical spirit.

Several recently launched theological journals show the extent of the creative thought within the churches. The new *Lutheran Quarterly* in America; *Theology Today* published at Princeton; the *Scottish Journal of Theology; Cross Currents,* which includes both Roman Catholic and Protestant articles; the Catholic *Ecumenist;* and the conservative evangelical *Christianity Today,* published at Washington, D.C. reflect the new theological mood. They demonstrate that it is possible to work theologically within a tradition and at the same time to keep the mind of the whole church as the vital context of theological reflection.

One important factor in this renewal of the vitality of particular traditions has been the re-examination of the original thought of the creative figures who stand at the source of our various traditions. The outstanding example is the Luther research carried out with extraordinarily vigorous scholarship in the past decades. The field is well reviewed by Edgar Carlson in his *The Reinterpretation of Luther.* Swedish scholars have been perhaps foremost in reinterpreting the reformer's doctrine. Anders Nygren's *Agape and Eros* and Gustaf Wingren's *Luther on Vocation* are outstanding works. This interest is by no means confined to the Lutherans. Two English Methodists, Phillip Watson in *Let God Be God* and Gordon Rupp in *The Righteousness of God,* have important Luther studies based on the new research. The Roman Catholic, J. Lortz's *Reformation in Deutschland,* offers significant revisions of the usual Catholic picture of Luther. Wilhelm Pauck has reviewed Lortz's book in an essay in *The Heritage of the Reformation.* In this and other essays in this volume Pauck shows the radical and creative elements in Luther's thought which have often been obscured by orthodox interpretation. He also shows how tendencies in Luther's thought later came to obscure the free and personal character which he assigned to knowledge of the word of God in Christ.

The Scottish theologian, Torrance, has done something similar for Calvin in his treatment of Calvin's conception of man. Torrance interprets Calvin's doctrine in relation to the emphasis on the personal relationship to God which Martin Buber and Emil Brunner have made the key to their thought about the difference between the Biblical and the rationalistic views of man. Torrance certainly communicates more of the living movement of Calvin's thought than most of the books which tended to identify Calvin with Calvinism, and thus miss the flexibility and deep sense of the personal nature of faith which he had.[18]

Methodist thought has received fresh inspiration from several new studies of John Wesley in which his divergence from Calvinism is recognized, but in which we are reminded how the major theme of sin and grace keeps Wesley close to Calvinism. Edward Ramsdell in *The Christian Perspective,* and Edwin Lewis show the strong influence of the emphasis on the distinctive character of the Biblical outlook. Georgia Harkness has enlarged the personalist tradition with a similar probing of basic Christian themes.

This theological activity, the extent of which we have barely suggested, displays a rich and complex pattern. There are many conflicts between traditions and within traditions, and the opening up of new possibilities which go beyond either traditional orthodoxy or self-confident liberalism. Amidst the cultural and intellectual ferment theological systems are being produced by some extraordinarily creative thinkers. There is Barth's monumental *Church Dogmatics,* Emil Brunner's *Dogmatics,* and Paul Tillich's *Systematic Theology.* Gustaf Aulen and L. Harold DeWolf have written one volume systematic theologies. On the Catholic side there is such creative work as Bernard J. F. Lonergan's *Insight,* Peter Schoonenberg's *God's World in the Making,* and the work of Karl Rahner which has been so important for Vatican II.

One looking from the outside at Christian theology today may decide that there is nothing in it but an ancient tradition defending itself against attacks, and seeking to perpetuate itself. Theology may appear to move like a glacier by its own inertia, cutting down the channel of history, breaking off in huge chunks whenever an outworn idea reaches a boundary where it can no longer he held within the main mass. But those who stand within the theological movement find it is not dead like a glacier, but rather alive in a community of people who share a common faith. It is the ongoing life of the Christian people responding to new demands which keeps theology from becoming a museum of antiquated ideas. The theologian can only share that life as he is given grace, and with the intellectual tools at hand seeks to give an ordered expression to the truths which make the Christian faith intelligible.

Theology which performs this service well does itself become at times the vehicle of God's word. Wherever God's truth breaks through to man, communicating the reality of life in the new community of forgiven sinners who live by faith, there the word of God is being spoken whether this comes through preaching, liturgy, action or theology. Theology stands on the boundary between the church and the wider community of men with their restless demand to know the whence and whither of life and the grounds of hope. Every Christian really lives on that boundary. In so far as he thinks about how his faith answers the human questions, every Christian is a theologian.

In the five following chapters we shall try to say how theologians today are dealing with five central problems in Christian thought.

CHAPTER II

The Bible and Christian Truth

CHRISTIAN thinking always comes back to the question, "How do we know our beliefs are true?" Real faith is marked by its own confession of a continuing struggle for truth. "Lord I believe, help thou mine unbelief," is a Christian prayer. Yet the prayer would be meaningless unless beyond the uncertainty there were some sure hold on truth. This strange position of the Christian believer between assurance and a continual struggle for truth is seen in all aspects of the Christian life. The light by which we see shines in Jesus Christ. Yet that light is always mixed with the shadows and lesser lights of our human groping. Its meaning must always be brought into some correlation with the truth of science, art and philosophy, and that work is never finished.

The Bible itself shows how the Gospel has been interpreted by making use of ideas drawn from many cultural sources. The Old Testament derives from Persian dualism its apocalyptic ideas of the world's end which come to play such a significant role in the time of Jesus. The writer of the Fourth Gospel is preaching to Greeks and he uses concepts such as Logos, Light of the world, and Eternal Life. He may indeed be giving these Greek terms a Hebraic meaning; but there is a mutual modification of the two outlooks as they meet each other. It is certainly true that fundamental elements in the Greek view of the world, such as the emphasis upon the realm of eternity above the realm of time, and the tendency to seek salvation through the ascent of the human spirit toward the mystical vision of the divine reality, were woven into the interpretation of the Christian faith which came to its first great synthesis in St. Augustine.

The question which troubles Christian thought is whether this fusing of the Gospel with philosophical reflection betrays the Gospel. The question may be put in slightly different form. Is the truth which the Bible gives us a truth which is prepared for by a more general disclosure of God throughout human experience, or does the truth of the Bible come as a revolutionary faith which stands sharply against all other human reflection about God however religious or idealistic that reflection may be?

I

We can divide Christian thinkers on this issue into two groups. The first says that the truth which we have in its fullness in the Biblical message is beginning to be known everywhere that men think seriously and rationally about their experience. The God we know in Christ has not left himself without witness anywhere. All man's religious experience has been a response to God's universal revelation. There is some light therefore in all profound religion which the Christian faith can accept as true. Buddha and Lao-tse, Aristotle and Plato grasped some fundamental insights into man and his relationship to the holy reality upon which his life depends. St. Thomas Aquinas believed that human reason can prove the existence of God. This is the official doctrine of the Roman Catholic Church. St. Thomas gave philosophical expression to the truth for which Paul contends when he says: "God himself has made it plain—for ever since the world was created, his invisible nature, his everlasting power and divine being, have been quite perceptible in what he has made."[1]

If we are to see this first viewpoint in its true proportions we must keep in mind that it does not claim that all the truth in the Christian faith can be derived from man's universal experience. There have been a few philosophers, Spinoza and Hegel for example, who have held that the whole of the Biblical truth can be expressed in philosophical terms. Since for them all religion can be given objective rational expression the question can be asked why there needs to be any special revelation at all. But this Hegelian position has never maintained itself successfully in the church. What can be strongly defended is the view that some real truth about God is available through man's experience in whatever culture or philosophical outlook he may be. God's holiness and power; something of his moral law; and, for some at least, a flickering consciousness of the divine love, are known outside of Christianity. Those who hold this always argue that unless God has revealed something of himself everywhere, the special and final revelation in Jesus Christ would be meaningless. It would find nothing in man as he is which it could quicken into active response. If it be replied that sinful man cannot recognize the true God, the answer is that it makes no sense to say men are sinners, that is willfully estranged from God, unless they have some knowledge of the God against whom they sin.

In contrast to this first position with its doctrine of the universality of man's awareness of God comes the stress on the scandal of the Gospel to the natural man. From Luther and Calvin to the present the radical upholders of this alternative view do not deny that God is really present and that he *could* be known everywhere in our experience. But the question is whether we do *actually* know God in his true holiness and love without the special aid of his personal self-disclosure in Jesus Christ.

True, men have thought about God in all cultures. Some of the ablest human minds have discussed God's being and his relation to the world. But does any human thought about God which proceeds without the resource of the Christian revelation arrive at the loving and caring God? Emil Brunner says it does not. Because human nature is corrupted by sin, all rational ideas of God are impersonal and legalistic.[2] Here is the heart of the issue.

If man's rational conception of God involves misunderstanding then we really cannot say he knows God in the sense that he knows what ought to be known in order to enter into the saving relationship which God offers in Christ. Even the knowledge of God's mercy in the Old Testament is put in a new light when in the New Testament God shows himself as actively seeking out the sinner to restore him to the circle of love. From this perspective all human religion and philosophy appears as falling into those "entangling alliances" with the man-created idols which serve our self-will. God is brought down to the level of some human special interest. Those who take this side of the discussion say that man cannot be saved from confusing his own sin-perverted ideals with the truth of God unless he sees through the Gospel light that God's truth is a judgment upon man's works. The true center of life is God's righteousness and not any human ideal.

There is for this second position one sense in which our experience does lead us toward God. This is the ironic sense that our attempt to lift ourselves toward God by our own mental and spiritual effort may drive us finally to confess our helplessness. To rely on anything other than God's freely given mercy brings us finally to the edge of that destruction which his wrath finally visits upon the proud. Self-centered concern is the secret poison eating away at the heart of our human self-confidence. The fact that we die is the most obvious reminder that life presents us with problems which we cannot solve. That is why for Christianity death becomes an ultimate symbol of the boundaries of human effort. So in this paradoxical way our self-trust may lead us toward God just because it leads us to the point where we may discover him who alone is to be trusted absolutely.

Finally, for those who stress this revolution which the Gospel brings into our life, it must be pointed out that the new relationship of faith does lead man to a right reason about God. Now we see in faith through a glass darkly, but now we really see. We cannot put the truth of the Gospel in such a way as completely to satisfy human logic. But we can reason about life and the world with a more adequate sense of the real meaning; because to be restored to our rightful mind means to know the limits of our human goodness. It is to know the depth of the alienation between man and God; and yet to know where this alienation is overcome. Therefore our reasoning within the life of faith ought to be free from the lifeless abstractions and mistaken pretensions of faithless reason. We should never suppose that any Christian is free from the temptation to claim to possess as his own a knowledge which only God can give. God's word judges all human words. This release which the Gospel brings to the mind is expressed in Luther's triumphant declaration: "This is the golden age of theology. It cannot rise higher; because we have come so far as to sit in judgment on all the doctors of the church and test them by the judgment of the apostles and prophets."[3]

Luther's reference to "prophets and apostles" is of course his assertion that the Bible is the source of the true word of God. So today when there is a marked turning toward a position close to Luther's the central problem revolves around the authority of the Bible. What is the relation of the truth of the Bible to human experience and reason? For is not the Bible also human words, and a reflection of human experience? Certainly the Bible is a product of human experience, whatever else it may be. And therein lies the crucial theological problem. What is the place of the Bible in our Christian knowledge of God? We shall examine some of the leading positions on this issue today.

II

Karl Barth's theology is a monumental achievement. His work has been a dominant factor in the theological scene since his *Commentary on Romans* in 1918, with its revisions through six editions.

His *Church Dogmatics* has grown to spectacular proportions. In 1958 eleven great volumes of nearly a thousand pages each have been published, as Barth comes nearer to the completion of the doctrine of reconciliation and the final themes. The power of his work lies not only in the brilliance of his dialectical skill, but especially in the uncompromising way in which he has reasserted the Reformation doctrine of salvation by grace through Jesus Christ. He has tried to show that the Christian faith is established on grounds which have nothing to do with "natural theology." He rejects any reliance on a supplemental or preparatory revelation appropriated in man's religious or philosophical quests. It is the place which Barth gives to the Bible which we must consider here. On this issue he holds that the evangelical faith stands against both Roman Catholicism and Protestant modernism, its two great rivals.

For Barth the Bible is one of the three forms in which the word of God is known to us. The revealed word of God is Jesus Christ. The Bible is the written word. That means it "becomes" the word when through it Jesus Christ is disclosed to us and we respond in faith. Third, there is the word of God as proclaimed in Christian preaching. Bible and preaching are dependent upon the essential word which is Jesus Christ. Now since the Bible is our original record and witness concerning Jesus Christ it is actually the norm for all statements of Christian belief. Barth declares "the absolute validity of the Bible as the Word of God, as the genuine, supreme criterion of Church proclamation and thereby also of dogmatics."[4]

Even as the word of God the Bible remains a human book written in human language. Barth acknowledges the right of the historical sciences to analyze, reconstruct and interpret the historical life out of which the Bible came. But all of this leaves for him the truth untouched that this book with all its human and fallible character is at the same time through God's grace his absolute word to us. "God's language is God's mystery." Of special importance is Barth's belief that the essential content of the Biblical faith is not in any way bound to the myths or the "world view" of the people from which it came. The Bible, he says, is free with respect to all "world pictures."[5] What it does contain for us is a truth which stands by itself. And this truth is just the grace of God in Jesus Christ. "The truth of Jesus Christ is not one truth among others; it is *the* truth, the universal truth that creates all truth as surely as it is the truth of God . . . to know Him is to know all."[6]

Barth develops this position which has been called "Christomonism" in his constructive theological system. The task of theology is to expound the Bible correctly. This means to understand the Biblical faith by seeing all of it from Jesus Christ as its one center and its essential content. The meaning of the covenant between God and man as developed in the Old Testament is understood by the Christian as a relationship which points forward to the covenant established in Christ. The meaning of creation is understood only when it is seen as the act of God through Christ. When Barth comes to the problem of the nature of time we might suppose he will have to take account of metaphysical problems as philosophers define them. If any problem seems to cry out for philosophy it is time. Not so for Barth. The Christian lives in the time determined by God's saving act in Christ. Our time in this era of grace is the time determined by the fact that Christ has risen from the dead. Barth seeks to penetrate through Biblical exegesis the meaning of this "new time" in which the risen Christ is really present among us. So he deals also with the meaning of our election to salvation. This ancient and knotty problem is handled by his holding that it is Jesus Christ who is the elect man. We are elected in him—not as separate individuals. Emil Brunner has criticized Barth's doctrine here as leading to an un-biblical conception of universal election and salvation. Whether Barth intends that outcome or not, he does set every problem of the Christian faith strictly within the relationship which God creates with man in Jesus Christ. We can see why he has apparently no need to go in any way outside the Bible to gain added truth or support for the Christian faith. The truth for the Christian is given in the Book and in the Man about whom the whole Book is written.

Behind this conception of Christian truth there lies Barth's doctrine of God which can be truly described as a radical assertion of the Reformers' theme of God's sovereignty. It is God's own will and choice that he reveals himself to us. We cannot hold his revelation or bind it to anything human. Barth goes a long way toward freeing the traditional meaning of sovereignty from the kind of static and deterministic form which it took in orthodox Calvinism. For Barth the key to God's nature is his freedom. He is the free Lord of all things manifesting himself in his Son, and communicating his word to us through his Holy Spirit. God as Father, Son and Holy Spirit is not "three beings in one." He is the one Holy God, free to communicate himself as he will. So Barth's systematic doctrine of revelation begins with an exposition of the doctrine of the Trinity. In this doctrine, he holds, the mystery of God's self-giving which underlies the whole Biblical faith is most adequately expressed.

Three things can be asked of any Christian theology. It must preserve and express the message of the Gospel. It should interpret the faith in a way which brings Christian belief into some kind of intelligible order with human knowledge and experience. Finally it should give an account of how faith may be presented to the unbeliever so that the way is opened for him to understand how it is related to his own experience. On all three counts Barth's theology stands impressively, but especially on the first two. Barth broke the Christian message away from a synthesis with modern culture which threatened to obscure its essential witness to God's judgment on all human works. He reasserts with the Reformers that the true health of human culture depends on the fundamental relation of the forgiven man to the forgiving God. It is plain that Barth desires to give an ordered account of the faith in relation to the whole range of human life and its problems. Man's ethical obligations, the mystery of his life and death, his struggles with anxiety and the possibilities of human comradeship and creation are all sensitively described by Barth.

A frequent criticism of Barth is that he leaves no place for apologetics, that is, for a meaningful discussion of the content of Christian faith with non-Christians. Even on this point it could be said that his uncompromising position, with its disillusionment about all human philosophy, may communicate more directly with the mood of sensitive people today than does the attempt to show that theology is "intellectually respectable," with its implied subservience to cultural norms. Barth's theology reasserts the form of the traditional Christian faith but its spirit is truly contemporary. Whoever knows man in his extremity will find Barth's theology speaking to his condition, even if he does not find Barth's answer wholly convincing.

The question which concerns us here has to do with what Barth does with the Bible. Does he rely as exclusively on the Bible witness as he claims to do? Is such an exclusive reliance possible? How is it that Barth is able to reinstate a theology which appears to be drawn from the ancient book, and yet remain a modern man who accepts modern science, with all the new understanding of the nature of the world that implies? The answer is that Barth must have some way of putting the "scientific" view of things in its proper place apart from the Biblical faith. He does have a way of doing this. Or better said, he relies upon another who found a way, Immanuel Kant. Barth has himself written that it was Kant who showed the eighteenth century the limits of its attempt by reason to understand the world. Barth's early theological development was within the framework of the Kantian philosophy with its sharp restrictions on metaphysical knowledge. Barth can take the attitude he does toward all human "world views" because he implicitly relies on Kant's Critical Philosophy with its limitation of scientific knowledge to the world of appearance. God lies wholly beyond our experience.

The question to Barth is that if one implicity relies on a philosophical orientation in order to make his theological case, does he not have to enter into philosophical discussion with those who hold a different point of view? Then human reason assumes a more positive and constructive role in theology than Barth allows.

The judgment that Barth has an implicit philosophy must take account of one further fact in his theological odyssey. He has himself said that the real turning point in his thought came with his book on Anselm of Canterbury, published in 1931. Now Anselm certainly did not hold the kind of restriction on human reason which Kant later did. Anselm developed the ontological argument for the existence of God which presupposes that man's reason can penetrate to the being of God himself. But notice that the key for Anselm is that all Christian understanding of God arises out of faith, and not apart from it. "Faith seeking understanding" is his formula for Christian thought. Once faith is presupposed, then the mind may begin to develop with a certain confidence the objective truth of God as that is made available through God's own self-revelation. If Barth has really passed beyond Kant's negative judgment on metaphysics back to Anselm's view that within faith reason may apprehend God, then the "scholastic" appearance of his dogmatic system becomes more understandable. Barth for example develops the doctrine of the Trinity, which can hardly be said to be set forth with any logical rigor in the Bible. Yet he makes the analysis of the Trinity the foundation of his whole dogmatic. This is hardly possible unless he believes that the faith-filled reason does lay hold of the very essence of God. He describes Christian knowledge as a kind of conformity to God's word through our being determined by that word.

In the later volumes of his *Dogmatics* Barth appears to many of his readers to be speaking more positively about the significance of human experience with its values of comradeship and creativity as reflections of the image of God in the human creature. Barth does indeed write of our existence in community, specifically in the order of male and female, as constituting the "image of God" in our finite being. He insists, of course, that this is an "analogy of relation" which has been established by God's free decision. It is not to be understood as a metaphysical analogy which would permit us to start with our experience and reason our way to knowledge of God. Barth has gone so far in his affirmation about this analogy of relation that Emil Brunner believes he must have altered his earlier position which, Brunner holds, denied any positive correlation between man's thought and God.[7] In the background of this discussion there is the controversy which Brunner has carried on with Barth over the question of whether in sinful man there remains any "point of contact" to which the Gospel can be addressed. For Brunner this "point of contact" is man's existence in responsibility. Thus the way is open for Brunner to work out the concept of personal encounter as the basis for Christian knowledge of God.

The issue here is a critical one for the interpretation of the Christian view of other religions, and indeed for every theology of culture. Is all knowledge of God to be denied outside the Christian revelation? Barth seems to say yes. Brunner says there is a revelation in the creation but outside of Christian faith men turn this revelation into an impersonal object. God is dimly known, but idols are put in his place. Other theologians equally concerned to preserve the uniqueness of Christianity insist that there must be some positive content in man's experience of God even though sin be presupposed. In *Our Knowledge of God* John Baillie has given a full account and a wise criticism of the Barth-Brunner controversy over the *imago dei*. Baillie holds that no man is ever without some real knowledge of God. An able review of the history of the doctrine of *imago dei* has been written by David Cairns. He stands close to Brunner's position, holding that there is an important Biblical basis for asserting God's universal fatherhood without depending exclusively on the New Testament doctrine of the new Image given in Jesus Christ. "Our endowment does go some way to constitute our continuing likeness to God; and this is purely an act of His grace to us."[8]

To return to Barth then, is it the case that he has no way of making a connection between the revelation in Christ and man's experience outside the Christian revelation? As his *Church Dogmatics* has developed, it begins to appear that Barth sees a solution in his Christologically centered doctrine. He has asserted that Jesus Christ is the whole meaning of human existence. Fortunately for readers who want to understand Barth here but are understandably daunted by the prospect of reading several thousand pages, he has written a very short essay, *Christ and Adam,* in which he condenses this most important theme of his theology. He expounds the fifth chapter of Romans in which Paul relates the story of Adam, the first and fallen man, to Jesus Christ, the man in whom the free gift of grace is given for all. What Barth finds here is the view that the story of Jesus is the story of the human race. At least from the standpoint of faith we can say that all life is bound together in the one reality we know in Him.

There, in Christ, is, for the first time in the true sense, the One who stands, as such, for all the others. He also is the Inaugurator, Representative, and Revealer of what through Him and with Him the many, *all* men shall also be, do, and receive. And there, also for the first time in the true sense, are the many, *all* men, not one of them less righteous or less blessed because he is not himself the One, but each rather finding and recognizing himself again in what this One who takes his place is, and does, and has received.[9]

It must be acknowledged that in his expounding of the meaning of Christ Barth has shown himself capable of illuminating a wide range of human experience. His analyses of anxiety and death, his exposition of the guilt of Judas, and his interpretation of the abyss of nothingness which yawns before the sinner offer penetrating disclosures of universal human themes. In a reflection on his early theology Barth has said that a more positive view of man is required and he has written an essay on *The Humanity of God*.

Emil Brunner is among the critics of Barth who say that any such relating of human experience to the revelation in Christ presupposes some analogy between human experience and the divine Word. For Brunner, as we have indicated, this analogy is found in the relationship of persons, the I-Thou relationship.[10] While Brunner believes that it is the Christian faith alone which fully recognizes the meaning of personal relationship, he acknowledges his indebtedness to the Jewish philosopher, Martin Buber's *I and Thou*. This book, with its less than a hundred meditative and evocative pages, has influenced contemporary theology as widely as has any single writing.

Buber draws a contrast between the personal relation in which both participants remain subjects, giving themselves to each other in freedom of the spirit, and the impersonal relation in which the other is a thing which I use, something determined, disposable, and existing only for my exploitation. This distinction is made the foundation of Brunner's theology. It has been worked out by Karl

Heim in his many writings including *The Transformation of the Scientific World-View* as a way of relating Christian faith to modern scientific theory. Heim analyzes the development of new concepts of spatial dimensions and relativity in modern physics and opens the way to the recognition of a personal dimension of space which can be used at least analogically as a basis for interpreting God's relationship to the world. H. Richard Niebuhr's book, *The Meaning of Revelation*, develops the personalistic position by distinguishing between our knowledge of "outer history," that is the history of objective events, and "inner history," that is the history of personal selves and their meanings. Niebuhr is not far from Barth in his skepticism about demonstrating the relation of Christian faith to universally valid principles. Paul Minear's work on Biblical Theology, *The Kingdom and the Power,* attempts to stay as closely as possible to the Bible's own message and its terms. But Minear does not rule out the importance of finding alternative means of expressing the faith which afford some way of communicating with those whose religious searching does not begin with the Bible.

III

Four schools of theology are ranged today against Barth's exclusive Biblicism. We begin with the thought of Rudolph Bultmann and Paul Tillich, because for them the issue with Barth is joined specifically at the point of how we are to understand the Bible today. Both Bultmann and Tillich believe that the forms in which the Gospel is interpreted today must take account of contemporary man's way of understanding his own existence. Both of them find such understanding expressed in existentialist philosophies.

We saw that Karl Barth separates the truth of Jesus Christ in the Bible from the "world view" of the Biblical writers. Bultmann, the New Testament critic and theologian, begins by raising the question, "What are we to do with the fact that the Bible is written within the framework of an ancient world view?" The Biblical writers thought of the world in the three-story structure of ancient supernaturalism. They thought of supernatural beings coming to this earth from above and from below. Angels and devils invade the human sphere. The Biblical account of even the most central matters of faith such as Jesus' temptation, crucifixion and resurrection are all involved in this account which has a mythical element. Bultmann means by myth the accounts of the appearance on this human plane of beings from the upper and lower worlds.

Bultmann says that before the Biblical message can be grasped in its truth for us today it must be "demythologized."[11] The positive content of the Gospel must be separated so far as possible from involvement with this mythical world view. To do this we must find in our own experience that basis of understanding with which the Gospel can really communicate. If we give up the notion of the three-story world, then some other way of saying what happens to us in Jesus Christ must be found. Bultmann adds weight to his argument by pointing out that in the Fourth Gospel itself the process of "demythologizing" has already begun. There concepts like "last judgement" and the miracles of the Christ story are given a spiritual meaning which is intelligible within a world view not dependent upon the mythical elements which are prominent in the Synoptic Gospels. Bultmann also stresses how Jesus in his own teaching dwelt much less on the details of the apocalyptic expectations concerning the end of the world than did the general religious thought of his day. Paul also spends little time trying to defend the literal interpretation of mythical elements in the tradition.

The argument of Bultmann here is not a new one. The entire development of modern Biblical criticism presupposes it. But he has acutely shown that the issue today cannot be formulated simply as to whether or not the Bible is the supreme authority for Christian faith. The real issue is, "How can we have the authoritative content of the Biblical message today when we must read the Bible with minds shaped by our modern understanding of the world?" "Demythologizing" is not a rejection of Biblical authority. It is for Bultmann the only way in which the Gospel can be set free from outworn beliefs and become truly authoritative for contemporary man.

The answer which Bultmann himself gives as to how the content of the Gospel can be related to our experience is derived from existentialist philosophy, especially from themes which Martin Heidegger has stressed. Man's creaturely existence with its encircling boundary line of death plunges him into an anxiety which he cannot overcome by any reliance on his own resources. Heidegger identifies this human state with guilt. Bultmann makes plain that it is guilt before God because it is refusal to accept our creaturely condition with gratitude to its giver. What man needs is the destruction of any understanding of himself which makes him rely on his own goodness or knowledge. He needs courage to venture into the unknown future in spite of all the threats to the meaningfulness of his life. The Gospel declares that God has overcome death and guilt. This is what the resurrection of Jesus Christ means. God offers man a new self-understanding in which life is lived from God as center. In that new life we have courage to face any future.

Bultmann's theological program has created a strong theological and philosophical reaction throughout the world. One collection of essays discussing the theme of "Kerygma and Myth," edited by Hans-Werner Bartsch, has expanded into six volumes including an entire volume of comment by Roman Catholic scholars. A score of books by theologians and philosophers has added to the debate.[12] In the later volumes of his *Dogmatics*, Karl Barth has taken account of Bultmann's assertion of the need for an existential interpretation of the Biblical message, and Bultmann has replied.[13] What is clear is that Bultmann has pointed unmistakably to the critical question concerning the place of the Scripture in Christian faith. How is the Scripture to be interpreted? The radical character of his answer has led to views ranging all the way from those which see him as dissolving the Gospel in the acids of modern skepticism to those which regard him as having found the one way to preserve the power of Biblical message, the *kerygma*, in the face of modern skepticism.

As this debate over "demythologization" has proceeded, it has become clear that the most important aspect of Bultmann's doctrine does not have to do solely with the question of the mythical element in the Bible. The more general and critical issue has to do with the relation between faith as spiritual assent and the objective structure of the beliefs which are required for faith. What Bultmann is proposing to do is to set the Christian believer free from any bondage to the requirement of assertion about scientifically defined facts or theories. He holds that if the believer must accept certain statements about what happened in history as, for example, in the resurrection narratives, in order to preserve the content of faith, then faith has become a new law imposed on the person. It should be emphatically said that Bultmann does not deny the existence of facts or that we live in a world of structures and principles. What he holds is that we cannot know the Gospel in its relevance to our age and every age if we demand that the Christian believer adhere to some objectively definable assertion about those facts and principles. It is the personal faith of the believer, his response to the spiritual reality of God communicated through the objective world, but transcending it, that is the absolute foundation of the believer's life.

The Roman Catholic critics are among those who see in Bultmann's position a strict application of the Reformation principle of salvation by grace alone. Nothing can be required of the believer but his personal assent to a spiritual Word. The Catholic asks, isn't this the real logic of the Reformer's principle?[14] It seems to abandon all objectivity. Unquestionably the critics here have penetrated to the heart of Bultmann's position, which is the radical freedom he assigns to faith. His existentialism appears to set aside the traditional questions which philosophers have discussed, the nature of being, the universal structures of the world, and concern about historical evidence. He would get along without the traditional systems of ontological structure which philosophy and religion have asserted. Man alone, responding in faith to the Eternal Word of God, is to be the sole theme. We turn now to Paul Tillich's theology, which stands in close relation to Bultmann's position, but in which there is a more complex attempt to relate personal faith to a doctrine about the nature of God's being and his relation to the world.

IV

If one takes up the first volume of Tillich's *Systematic Theology* and looks at it side by side with Barth or with Brunner's *Dogmatic,* they appear as different as night from day. Where Barth and Brunner depend upon continued reference to Biblical sources and work out theology in closest relation to a systematic Biblical exegesis, Tillich's work seems filled with philosophical terms. He discusses God only after he has clarified the metaphysical meaning of being and nonbeing. He discusses sin in relation to an existential analysis of anxiety. Anxiety is interpreted in relation to the metaphysical structures of space, time, causality and substance. This weaving together of theology and philosophy is the key to Tillich's method. His aim is to produce an apologetic theology which will bring the Christian message into specific relation with the ways in which contemporary man understands his experience.

Tillich's solution of the problem of apologetics is to develop what he calls the method of "correlation." This means that the Gospel is to be shown to give answers to the questions which man asks in his attempt to find the meaning of life. We cannot look to philosophy for the real truth about God or the way of salvation.

"The problem of correlation cannot be solved by another attempt to build a natural theology. Human existence does not involve answers to the question of man's relation to God; it involves the question."[15]

What the theologian has to do is to show how man's existence as a finite creature drives him to the question of ultimate being, that is to the question of God. Man's existence in anxiety raises the question of a courage which can overcome anxiety. Man's ultimate concern to know the infinite reality beyond his finite existence raises the question of a final revelation which judges all preliminary grasp of the divine.

The norm for Christian thought then cannot be found in philosophy or in any other kind of human resource. It is given to the Christian in the final revelation in Jesus Christ. But we see how the method of correlation puts the problem of the norm in a new way. The meaning of Jesus Christ cannot be stated in Biblical terms alone. It must be stated as the answer to the questions raised by human philosophical and religious searching. Both the form of the question and the form of the Christian answer are determined in part by the form in which the question is asked. This is why Tillich's systematic theology is so heavily freighted with a philosophical analysis of the structure of being. As theologian he interprets man's life philosophically in order to show how the Christian message overcomes that separation between man and God which all philosophy reveals. The one literal statement man can make about God takes a philosophical form. God is "being itself."

Jesus Christ is the final revelation. We need then to say explicitly how he is the norm for theology, and especially how that norm is related to the Biblical message. Here Tillich departs from Barth's doctrine that the Bible itself becomes the final norm. This, he holds, restricts theology in a way which makes it impossible for the Biblical message to become meaningful for succeeding generations. It tries to freeze the norm, but actually "the norm grows."[16] We have to grasp God's truth in Christ through a continual reappropriation in new historical situations. The Biblical message must be correlated with our human questions as we ask those questions at a given time. For Tillich, therefore, the norm of theology for our situation today must be stated in terms which make explicit how the Gospel speaks to the condition of man in his estrangement and anxiety. Tillich calls the norm of theology the "New Being." To live in Christ is to participate in a new creation. In this new life "the self-estrangement of our existence is overcome." It is a reality of "reconciliation and reunion, of creativity, meaning, and hope."[17]

This statement of the theological norm does not mean a rejection of the authority of the Bible. For Tillich, it saves the authority of the Bible by relating its message to the concrete situation in which men read the Bible. Where then do we get our formulation of the questions we must have answered? We have to turn to the philosophies or other interpretations of the human situation. Tillich recognizes that we would not ask our questions in the way we do if the Christian faith had not already shaped our minds and our culture. Not even the attackers of Christianity like Nietzsche, perhaps they least of all, can escape the fact their spirits have been molded by the Christian heritage. Still our questions are real questions, for man must ask who he is and what his existence means. The formulation of the question is done by philosophers, artists and plain folk who give some explicit voice to their human concerns. When he formulates the ultimate questions, Tillich as theologian does not invade the territory of the philosopher to argue with him; but he does have a philosophical orientation. It is derived from the mystical tradition in Jacob Boehme and Friedrich Schelling, from the existentialism of Schelling's later philosophy and from Kierkegaard. There are numerous other influences including Hegel, Marx and the new psychology; but it is fair to say that Tillich stands closest to the perspective of the existentialist movement. Man's existence in finitude is existence in "ontological anxiety." Death and guilt are, when profoundly understood, the twin symbols of man's two ultimate problems; his anxiety about the "end" of his life and his anxiety about his spiritual isolation from God. Tillich draws upon Kierkegaard, and the later existentialists, upon modern literature and art, especially painting, to express the way in which contemporary man struggles to find salvation. His theological method leads him to look beneath the ideologies and conflicts of our culture to uncover the spiritual unrest that is there, and to show what it means. Tillich's power to penetrate to the deeper levels of the human spirit where man's anguish breaks his self-confidence and leads him to the question of God is the secret of the evocative power of his writing. The Biblical message becomes authoritative when it is shown how it brings light into our darkness.

Tillich's thought stands in a place of decisive importance in the theological situation because he proposes a reconciliation of modern man's search for meaning and the Christian faith without returning to a dogmatic biblicism. The second volume of his *Systematic Theology* was published in 1957, with a third volume to follow. In this orderly, intricate, and powerful work, as well as in his sermons and the widely read *The Courage to Be,* Tillich shows that he can elicit an understanding of the significance of the Christian faith even from those who stand entirely outside it, because he holds together in a delicate synthesis so many strands of human thought, experience, and religious insight.

His alliance with existentialism, for example, does not cause Tillich to abandon the philosophical search for the structure of being. This distinguishes his theological method from Bultmann's. Idealism as a philosophy wove a veil over the face of nineteenth-century culture and hid its conflicts; but the idealists' search for ontological reality expressed a fundamental aspect of human life, and faith cannot set it aside. The idealists indeed knew of man's estrangement from God and from himself, but they believed that this could be overcome through theoretical analysis and historical progress. It is this illusion which the existentialists have penetrated.

In Boehme and Schelling Tillich finds the expression of that mysticism which asserts the reality of freedom in the life of God himself. There is an eternal process of separation and reunion in the depth of the divine which is the ground both of the creativity and the anxiety which we finite creatures experience. Knowledge of this depth of freedom and the reconciliation which is brought about through grace cannot be completed by objective reason. It must come through a mystical transformation in which the depth of the self is grasped by the divine. Therefore the verification of religious belief can never be restricted to scientific methods of analysis alone. There is a kind of verification in the living process of experience. We come to a boundary beyond which our rational insight cannot go; but at that boundary we may begin to discover our true origin and destiny. This religious knowledge is "receiving" knowledge which has its own validity. It complements and does not destroy our scientific, "controlling" knowledge.

Since this theology stresses that there must be preparation for new insight, we are within its spirit if we ask what preparation there has been in American thought to appreciate Tillich's work. We remember that we have had a strong influence from German idealism through the Transcendentalist movement by way of Emerson and Coleridge. Hegel's philosophy created its own American school in the latter part of the nineteenth century. Josiah Royce and William Ernest Hocking form a distinguished and continuous tradition of Hegelian idealism to the present day. Personalistic idealism from Bowne to Brightman would fall under Tillich's strictures against "rationalism" and yet its view is not far from his. Further we should remember the romantic element in the American spirit as nurtured in part by idealism. On working through Tillich's persuasive account of our knowledge of God one may well recall Walt Whitman's Democratic Vistas with its rough-hewn but probing expression of the yearning of the spirit: "What is I believe called idealism seems to me to suggest (guarding against extravagance, and ever modified even by its opposite) the course of inquiry and desert of favor for our New World metaphysics, their foundation of and in literature, giving hue to all." Whitman has his own existential realism. He calls for great poems of death. "The poems of life are great; but there must be great poems of the purpose of life, not only in itself but beyond itself."[18] Tillich's theology is more than a romantic yearning. It is a realistic account of how man feels when he has come to the very edge of despair, and can find no meaning in life unless there comes a healing disclosure from beyond himself. Beginning with the doctrine that "being is finite, existence is self-contradictory, and life is ambiguous," Tillich's theology communicates the Christian word of renewal in a way which combines the Bible's message with the thought forms of man today.)

V

Another attempt to work out a theology in which the Biblical message is integrated with a philosophical outlook is made by theologians who follow Alfred N. Whitehead. The development in the theological faculty at the University of Chicago led by Henry N. Wieman and developed on the philosophical side by Charles Hartshorne is an attempt to work out a Christian theology through a positive use of Whitehead's doctrine that process rather than timeless being is the ultimate metaphysical truth. Whiteheadians argue that the traditional notion of God as complete in his being and beyond all change is a self-contradictory idea which forms no necessary part either of an adequate metaphysics or a sound Christian theology. In *Man's Vision of God* and *The Divine Relativity*, Hartshorne has argued this point with great logical skill and religious insight. He retains and restates the classic ontological argument for the existence of God as the most perfect being. He has elaborated a metaphysical vision of God whose essence is love, and who eternally completes himself by entering into reciprocal relations with his creatures. They depend upon him, yet they have their measure of freedom in the ongoing process which is the concrete life of the universe conceived as a dynamic society with God its supreme member.

Dr. Wieman, who emphasizes the empirical strand in Whitehead's and Dewey's philosophies, approaches the knowledge of God through identifying in human experience that observable process which works beyond human control and planning, and which is the creative source of human good. This process is social intercommunication of qualitative meanings, that is, concrete personal appreciations. Wieman does not elaborate the metaphysical structure as do other Whiteheadians. But he describes the creative and saving work of God in such a way as to stress God's sovereign initiative over human desires. Whitehead's vision of God as primordial structure and as consequent experience does not so clearly show what God's function as saving power in history may be. In *The Source of Human Good* Wieman elaborates a distinction between God as "creative good" and the "created goods" which God's working achieves. Christian devotion is to the "creative good" as sovereign over all. Here Wieman joins a high Calvinist theological vision to a radical emphasis on direct experience as the basis of religious knowledge.[19]

Neither Wieman nor those who draw inspiration from his work offer religious philosophy as a substitute for Christian faith. Rather they hold that the philosophy of process can give a more adequate interpretation of the Bible's account of God's creative and redemptive action than can the idealistic philosophical tradition. Idealism, when it is impersonalistic, makes God an impassive absolute, remote from the world's agony, or it identifies him with the whole process of being, and thus has all the unsolved problems of a monism in which evil cannot have any intelligible place. The God of the Bible engages in historical action and his creatures have real though limited freedom. Bernard M. Loomer's essay, "Christian Faith and Process Philosophy," Bernard Meland's *The Re-Awakening of Christian Faith,* and Daniel Williams' *God's Grace and Man's Hope,* along with Harold Bosley's writings have tried to show how the Biblical message comes into a positive relationship to our contemporary understanding of the world when we see the Bible's faith in the God who works here and now in our history.

Critics of this school raise all the questions which are directed against any "natural theology." Certainly the task of showing that the new metaphysical outlook can really illuminate our understanding of the Biblical experience is very much itself in "process." It has yet to be thoroughly worked out. It can also be fairly said that metaphysicians like Whitehead have had far less to say about the tragic character of man's life and his sin, than have the existentialist philosophies. On the other hand the process thinkers charge that existentialism breaks up human processes into disconnected moments of decision. It fails to make sense out of a real historical continuity in God's work of creation and redemption, whereas the Bible always has in view the history of God's working from age to age.

Dr. Nels Ferré's growing and impressive theological doctrine may well be taken account of here, for Ferré is also deeply influenced by Whitehead. But in contrast to the Chicago school he strikes out on his own lines to work out an independent philosophical preface to his exposition of the Christian faith. The key to Ferré's thought is his attempt to keep the element of process in his view of God and yet to assert that there is in God a higher order of being which is not subject to the limitations of existential processes. For Ferré, God combines the ideal and the actual. He is absolutely sovereign, and will in the end really save all things. This outcome is not known by reason. Reason would have to accept Whitehead's restrictions on God's sovereign power. We know it by faith. Ferré believes he can hold together the world of actual experience with its flux, its struggles between good and evil, and the idea of God's transcendence over all limitation. God is love, and that love must mean a continual and eternal creative working. Thus Ferré gets the dynamic element into God's nature. God's perfect love is precisely that which leads him forever to create. Ferré seems here close to the traditional view as held by St. Thomas Aquinas. He does make explicit use of the doctrine also held by Aquinas that we must always move by analogy from human experience to project our thought beyond experience into the nature of God. Ferré's is certainly one of the boldest attempts in modern thought to give a philosophical rationale to the Christian faith. One is more than a little hesitant to characterize it because as a system it too is "in process." But its spirit surely looks toward the uniting of the Gospel theme that God is love with an attempt to understand the whole of our experience by seeing it in this perspective of faith.[20]

VI

If we deal even more briefly with Anglican and Roman thought it is not that the theme of Biblical faith and its relation to human reason is any less important to theologians working today in those traditions. Far from it. Rather it is these traditions which have always worked toward a discriminating and elaborate synthesis between faith and reason. For all Augustinians "faith seeks understanding." Roger Hazelton's *Renewing the Mind* is a discerning statement by a Protestant theologian of this view of faith and reason. For Thomists "faith completes understanding." For both schools faith can never destroy reason nor exist satisfactorily without its aid.

Anglican theology today moves with its wonted balance, complexity and serenity. It continues to be congenial to philosophical developments which can be integrated into the Christian structure with God's incarnation as the crown of his cosmic work of creation and redemption. The late Archbishop Temple's works, Father Thornton in *The Incarnate Lord,* Leonard Hodgson in his work on the Trinity all make use of Whitehead's metaphysics with its theory of the evolutionary process moving toward new levels of complexity and value. But all of these allow the Whiteheadian world view only to look upward toward the Incarnation. Only the Word made flesh as it is disclosed to faith can complete the Christian understanding of our being.

Alan Richardson's *Christian Apologetics* is an analysis of the sense in which theology can be both a science, and yet go beyond all human science. Richardson holds that theology has its own distinctive datum in revelation. Knowledge that it is God who speaks in the event of revelation is given only to faith. Now revelation means essentially illumination. Here Richardson makes full use of the Augustinian metaphor of light. God enlightens our minds to give us knowledge. In the light of faith, we see truth. This introduction of a faith principle which guides reason is not something peculiar to Christianity. Every world view whether Marxist, Freudian or positivist does the same, Richardson says. The Christian faith principle is drawn from the Biblical revelation. "Man comes to the knowledge of the truth, not by the untrammeled exercise of his reasoning powers, but by accepting or being given the faith which enables him to use his reason aright."[21] Once it has established this priority of faith, theology needs to show that the Christian faith can more completely deal with all the facts than can any other. Here is the basis for apologetics. We discuss with others who hold other faith principles, but we do not assume that any serious thought is neutral. Every faith involves some key principle by which it organizes its world.

The increasing attention being given to studies in Biblical theology is reflected in Anglican theology today. Father Thornton's detailed studies of the nature of the church and of revelation in the Bible are examples. Father Hebert traces the development of the worshiping community in the Old Testament and the New, in his *The Throne of David* and *The Form of the Church*. Michael Ramsey in his *The Gospel and the Catholic Church* and his study of the resurrection shows how the faith and form of the church arise from the original witness to the Gospel.

Roman Catholic theology has always rejected the exclusive Biblicism of some Protestant theology. The *Summae* of St. Thomas Aquinas are still the officially accredited expositions of Catholic philosophy as the recent encyclical *Humani Generis* reaffirms. But this encyclical was written just because in the view of Pope Pius XII there has been such a strong movement which looks less to St. Thomas than to existentialist philosophy in order to relate the Catholic faith to present-day thought. Gabriel Marcel is one outstanding Catholic thinker who has stressed the unique character of personal existence (and the necessity for a fresh interpretation of the nature of personal faith. Marcel does not simply echo existentialist doctrine. His philosophical writings and his plays written before existentialism became "popular" worked out many of the themes which existentialism now emphasizes. Marcel puts vividly the key and temper of this dynamic Catholic thought:

> Every genuine and personal relationship is really a way into that growing and living community to which Christian theology gives the name of the Mystical Body. This is precisely the point where mere Theism necessarily points beyond itself and where Revelation begins; but I am of course intimately convinced that revelation cannot be considered as something which is brought, so to say, as a fire-ball falling on our mental planet. There is on the contrary every reason to believe that Revelation is the crowning of an immense cosmic travail which at one and the same time calls it forth and implies it as its internal source.[22]

Father D'Arcy's *The Mind and Heart of Love* shows clearly the desire to enrich the Thomist doctrine of the self by emphasizing the ecstatic and self-sacrificing tendencies which exist in tension with the self-realizing tendencies St. Thomas emphasizes. D'Arcy makes special use of a study by another Roman Catholic, Hunter Guthrie, which draws widely upon contemporary philosophies, and especially upon the existentialist analysis of anxiety to establish its thesis that the movement of our life is "not toward a truth to be possessed, but toward an end to be accomplished, not toward the sterile contemplation of the Absolute, but toward the love which is filled with self-giving."[23] *Humani Generis* apparently intends to put a radical restriction on such attempts to work out a new philosophical setting for the faith. The liberal Roman Catholic *Commonweal* declares that many of those who have come under this condemnation have been doing the most to make the

Catholic faith intelligible and persuasive for the contemporary mind.[24]

VII

We see that the Christian mind moves in diverse ways in its attempts to set forth its faith and its philosophy. It probably always will. There is one development in the schools of thought we have just examined which, while it does not point to any simple agreement, does represent an important advance over much traditional theology in all the various Christian bodies. In brief this is the new understanding of what revelation is, and of how the revelation we have through the Bible is related to the rest of human thinking about God. What has happened is that revelation as the "self-disclosure of God" is understood as the actual and personal meeting of man and God on the plane of history. Out of that meeting we develop our formulations of Christian truth in literal propositions. This means that revelation is interpreted in such a way as to reject the legalistic and dogmatic absolutizing of verbal formulas. Revelation is disclosure through personal encounter with God's work in his concrete action in history. It is never to be identified with any human words which we utter in response to the revelation. In *Nature, Man and God* William Temple described revelation as "intercourse of mind and event, not the communication of doctrine distilled from that intercourse." And he went on, "Knowledge of God can be fully given to man only in a person, never in a doctrine, still less in a formless faith, whatever that might be."[25]

Nearly every analysis of the problem of Christian truth which we have mentioned in this chapter would be in agreement with this statement. Barth, Tillich, the Whiteheadian school and the new Catholic personalism stress its importance. H. Richard Niebuhr's *The Meaning of Revelation* is an especially concise statement of the point. What it means is that Christian thought can be set free from the intolerable dogmatism which results from claiming that God's truth is identical with some human formulation of it. It gives freedom for critical re-examination of every Christian statement in the light of further experience, and in the light of a fresh encounter with the personal and historical act of God in Christ.

Even this theory of revelation is subject to criticism. The Anglican Farrer has sharply criticized the thesis that God "speaks personally to us" in his book, *The Glass of Vision*. He rightly emphasizes that the idea of God's speaking is hardly simple and clear in itself. But Farrer shows, in the present writer's judgment, that he is not free from the intellectualist errors which the personalistic school is criticizing when he holds that revelation is to be identified with "supernatural mysteries speaking through living images."[26] These images such as "Trinity," "Israel," "Kingdom of God," "dying and rising with Christ" are the indispensable ingredients of revelation. We ask, "Why are not these images just as subject to the fallibilities of man's apprehension of God as are propositional expressions?" Farrer is not unaware of this problem. Both his work and Father Thornton's new book on *Revelation* show that the discussion of the meaning of revelation can go on at a new level; and one has a right to believe at a much more profound level than it has in past quarrels over the verbal inspiration of the Bible or the infallibility of dogmatic pronouncements.

Most, though not all, of those who interpret revelation in this new perspective will also agree that God discloses himself in some way through all human experience. Revelation is not confined to the Christian strand of history even though it finds its climax and final definition there. The exploration of man's religious experience in all its forms which was widely developed through the period of liberal Christian thought has continued. Its positive significance for our fuller knowledge of God is widely stressed.

The works of the late Archbishop Söderblom, Rudolph Otto, Van Der Leeuw and Joachim Wach's studies in the history of religions all have definite bearing on the question of the relation of Christianity and the non-Christian religions. They all share the conviction that Christianity can retain the distinctive character of its own faith without taking a purely negative attitude toward religious experience outside of Christianity. Added emphasis on the importance of looking within man's experience for the inescapable structures which bind his life to God comes from interpreters of the new psychology. David Roberts has written:

> The structure of reality links misery and conflict to man's failure to reach a position where he can affirm his *whole* self; and it links beatitude to honesty and wholeness. Hence faith in God can rest upon actualities that function in existence here and now. . . . In theological language our conception of salvation definitely involves acceptance of the doctrine of divine immanence.[27]

If we say that revelation means God's disclosure to us of himself as the creator and redeemer of our life, and if we say that there is the possibility of revelation throughout human experience, then we seem to have made revelation a general category. Does this destroy what is distinctive about the Christian faith? What becomes of the authority of the Bible? One of the impressive things about the contemporary discussion is that this problem is clearly seen. It is being shown convincingly, I believe, that to admit revelation as in some sense universal does not lead to a denial of the distinctive character of the Christian revelation. Actually the term "general revelation" is misleading. Revelation is always special for it always comes to particular men in particular situations in history. It does not come as an abstract and universal truth out of history.

In the Christian revelation we know God as he has addressed us through the prophets and in Jesus Christ. In Christ we see God's own truth finally become luminous as it has nowhere else. Here the scattered fragments of our human apprehension of God receive a decisive judgment, and a new meaning. Now we see what God is through the form of a human life which is completely given in his service and in ours. But see now what this means for our conception of revelation. We understand revelation not only from the standpoint of general religious experience; but as Christians we see revelation in a new way. It means that kind of self-disclosure which God has given in Christ. As Christians we not only look at Christ from the standpoint of revelation; but we look at revelation from the standpoint of Christ. It is this fact for which Karl Barth's theology stands. In so far as those who stress revelation outside the Biblical experience tend to forget this truth, what Barth is contending for will always be a warning signal for theology. Against Barth what has to be said is that the Christ of the Bible comes as the fulfillment of the meaning of all life. He is the incarnation of the universal Logos. The Bible itself leads us to look everywhere in man's experience for some preparatory apprehension of the truth which in Jesus Christ has become decisively and personally available to us with that measure of fullness which is appropriate to us as finite creatures.

In concluding this chapter we need only to recall that this issue of authority which may seem somewhat abstract is a matter of life and death for the church. It is the question of the criterion by which we can be set free from the idols which call so insistently to our pride-filled spirits. This issue becomes all the more pressing in the new turn in theology where a radical question about our knowledge of God has become the center of attention. To that question we now turn.

CHAPTER III

God and the World

BETWEEN the years 1960 and 1965 a radical new turn has occurred in theology. Whitehead says that climates of thought last about thirty years. This would roughly cover the period we have called the "renaissance in theology" from about 1930 to 1960. During this period the Barthian movement achieved its wide influence. The reaffirmation of the reformation theme of justification by faith was made by Emil Brunner, by Reinhold and Richard Niebuhr and by Paul Tillich in major theological constructions. The decisiveness and uniqueness of the Christian revelation was given a biblical and theological interpretation which seemed to find for theology its proper autonomy with its own foundation and criterion.

The change in the present situation is not a radical discontinuity with what has gone before; but its dominant note is the reexamination of the problem of truth in the context of Christian faith. There seems much less assurance of how the work of theology is to be done. There is a radical questioning of traditional forms of doctrine. A new theological style seems in the making which is less concerned with the construction of systems and has a more radical sense of the problematic character of all human language about God. The task of theology, the articulation of the faith of the church goes on, but the context is shaped by a situation which requires some new approaches to every traditional mode of thought.

The appearance within Christian theology of radical doubt about the possibility of any authentic speech about God, a trend which is sometimes called the "death of God" movement in theology is but symptomatic of the disclosure that there is at the center of the theological task the question of how the Christian faith in God is related to the life of the twentieth century man, whose problems and whose hopes are largely determined by the rise of scientific technology. Assertions about God's action upon the world, and about the normative character of the biblical revelation are made in a world whose primary concern is mastering, using, and fulfilling the promise in the new powers available to man, and avoiding the destruction which the weapons of the atomic age can bring about. What is the relation of the structure of Christian faith in God's grace and his saving work in history to the new world picture, and this new shape of human affairs? We have already seen how Bultmann's question about the mythological element in the biblical record has pointed to a critical issue, and it is around Bultmann and his school that much of the contemporary theological turn has occurred in Europe. In Britain and America the philosophical tradition is not so confined to existentialism as on the continent, but here also the critical issue for theology is how to give a coherent meaning to belief in God in relation to the new understanding of the world.

We would do less than justice to the new turn in theology however if we centered attention exclusively on the intellectual problems, crucial as they are. We recognize that the theologies of the first half of the century were hammered out in first hand engagement with the political situations created by the Nazi idolatry, and by the World Wars. But the period at the beginning of the second half of the century presents a much more complex set of issues for mankind. The present era is characterized by unprecedented world political ferment. The threat of atomic destruction, the ominous wave of the population explosion, the passions of self-determination in the emerging new nations, the technological developments and urbanization all form the context of the world wide political revolution, with marxist, nationalist, capitalist and democratic forces contending with one another. In this situation the traditional religious communities have had their own renewal. They confront one another, but they also confront a human community which is breaking the bonds of every tradition with much violence, disorder, and suffering. We must look at some of the complex strands in this new context in which theological work must be done.

I

It may be said that it was an extraordinary phenomenon in the religious publishing world which gave the first clear public indication that the theological discussion was to undergo a transformation. A Bishop of the Anglican Church, John Robinson, himself a biblical scholar, published in 1963 a fairly brief book entitled *Honest to God* in which he raised in a frank way some questions about what it means to believe in God in the twentieth century. An unprecedented 350,000 copies were printed in a short time and the book has been the focus of an extraordinary theological discussion not only among theologians but throughout the church and culture.[1]

The theme of Bishop Robinson's book was not unusual in modern theology. He said that we must reconsider God's relationship to the world in the light of the way we understand the world through modern science. Traditional supernaturalism had a three-storied view of the world with God "up there." Later philosophical theology tried to preserve the understanding of God's being with the view of God as "out there" in the realm which transcends the finite. But Robinson said that neither of these gives us a satisfying answer as to how we can think of God's being. He turned to the theologies of Tillich and Bultmann, and appropriated Tillich's phrase in which God is encountered as the depth or ground of being. Robinson's presentation of this ontological outlook, and his stress upon personal encounter as Bultmann interprets faith was not in itself startling or revolutionary. What then explains the impact of his book? Undoubtedly the fact that a Bishop of the Church was writing thus frankly about his theological questioning was encouraging to many who had felt that the theologians were not asking their questions. But the real significance of Robinson's discussion lay not in the putting forward of the ideas of Tillich and Bultmann but at two special points which have become important in the new discussion.

First, he raised the question about God in a way which pointed to the unsettled question which remains even in the theologies of Tillich and Bultmann, "How does God act in the world?" If we believe in scientific laws, and the natural course of events how can we conceive the influence, the leading, and the intervention of God in this order? Must we have a new way of understanding what we mean when we say God is present, or that he acts? In the second place Bishop Robinson raised questions about the form of the religious life. He explored the conception of a "worldly Christianity" in which man no longer experiences religious emotion as authentic or as giving him special access to God. Robinson spoke for the man who has "come of age" in a world where he knows his own powers and limits, and faces his problems as one who accepts the natural order and makes his way within it without help from some special religious resource.

These two themes, God's being, and the new secularism, were found by Bishop Robinson in the later writings of Dietrich Bonhoeffer, the Christian theologian, martyred under the Nazis, and whose theological writings, brief and sometimes fragmentary as they are, have become one of the most powerful influences on present theological thought. It is important to see the direction Bonhoeffer's reflections were taking as he wrote the last letters from prison.

Dietrich Bonhoeffer was born in 1906. He grew up in the tradition of the Lutheran Church of Germany. He came to America to study as one rooted in that tradition yet one who had been influenced by Karl Barth and was striking out on independent lines. His doctoral dissertation, *The Communion of Saints*, was presented to the Theological Faculty of the University of Berlin in 1927. It showed Bonhoeffer's search for the distinctive theological reality of the Church yet with a concern for relevance to sociological and empirical understanding of human communities. Significantly he criticizes both Kierkegaard and Barth as not laying sufficient foundation for the fully personal and social relationship involved in the love of neighbor as understood in Christianity. This reaction against an extreme individualism remains characteristic of Bonhoeffer's thought to the end.

Another early work was his *Act and Being* in which he sought to establish the distinctive Christian understanding of God. He recognizes that there are philosophical problems which have to be taken into account when we speak of the being of God and say that God creates, acts, and redeems. It is again significant that while Bonhoeffer does not return formally to this problem in his writings, one of his most suggestive comments in the last days is directed to the question of how we are to conceive God's action in or upon the world, the issue which Bishop Robinson finds so important in the new theological reflection.

We turn then to consider the most important themes which Bonhoeffer suggested in his last writings, his *Letters from Prison*.[2] It is well to remember that these were brief suggestions about many topics. Most had been anticipated earlier, but here they reach a sharpness of definition. Bonhoeffer clearly was seeking a new way of grasping the message of the Christian faith so that it could be articulated for contemporary man.

First, he says, man is a social being and the authentic Christian life is life in the church. Bonhoeffer remarks that he is not concerned with "individual salvation" and he does not believe that contemporary man finds meaning in seeking the salvation of his individual soul. Bonhoeffer seems to equate individual salvation here with other-worldliness and concern about heavenly bliss. In any case, he expresses his sense of solidarity with the human family, and the conviction that the Gospel has to do with God's redemption of the world through the community which is being constituted his *ecclesia,* his church.

Second, Bonhoeffer moves toward the conception of a "worldly Christianity" in which the decisive categories for understanding the Christian life are not those which oppose the religious to the secular or non-religious, but those which declare the service of Christ as work in the world without appeal to special kinds of feeling, or symbols which can be designated as religious.

This view that Christianity is not primarily to be understood as a religion, but that it is a personal faith which transcends religious categories had indeed been a familiar theme of the theological renaissance. Barth, Brunner, Hendrick Kraemer, had all tried to show how in a right understanding of the revelation in Christ the "religious" categories are transcended. It is interesting that this idea appears in the 1927 dissertation when Bonhoeffer is discussing the Church:

> Essentially Jesus Christ was no more a founder of the Christian religious community than he was the founder of a religion. . . . He brought, established and proclaimed the reality of the new mankind. . . . This was not a new religion seeking adherents, which is a picture drawn by a later time.[3]

This theme recurs in the *Letters* in the vision of Christian life as "holy worldliness." Bonhoeffer moved toward the view that Christ is to be found and served wherever humanity is, and that the Christian has in a way to disappear into the world of men and affairs to find that real point of meeting with the other which is the authentic Christian concern.

Third, there is the now famous phrase about man's "coming of age." Bonhoeffer declared that contemporary man has come to such a mastery of his environment that he finds he can very well get along without appeal to any power beyond himself in solving the ordinary problems of human living. Man today turns to scientific agriculture for food, to medicine and surgery in dealing with disease, to human resources in meeting the demands of political existence. It is particularly striking that Bonhoeffer wrote in this vein while he was a prisoner of one of the most terrible of human tyrannies. But he saw beyond the pathology of the Nazi mentality to the self-confident spirit of modern man with his technological equipment. Man's "coming of age" means the attainment of that secular and scientific view of the world which leads him to look to rational human effort rather than any superior power or wisdom for achieving the life he wants to live.

Here then the question about God is raised by Bonhoeffer in a new context. It is not enough to affirm the Christian revelation with its biblical witness. The question is how this abyss between man's self confident attack on his problems and the traditional belief in man's dependence on God is to be understood. How can God be "pointed to" for man who has come of age? What kind of affirmation is Christianity making when it says that it is God who redeems the world and gives life its true meaning? We see that a new apologetic situation for theology is here recognized. The question is not whether we can find arguments for believing in God; but whether or not we can exhibit the relevance of faith in God. Bonhoeffer suggests that we must seek a new language in which to speak about God for the old language may not be expressing anything that contemporary man can hear. This situation of seeking a "new language" for the communication of faith has become especially emphasized in the new theological turn. It marks a break with the exclusive biblicism of the Barthian theology in which the affirmation of faith in strictly biblical terms was taken to be the key to theological method. Now it is seen more clearly that the communication of the meaning of the biblical witness may require new forms of speech which create bridges between the biblical language and the language of man in this new culture.[4]

There are two important suggestions by Bonhoeffer concerning the problem of language. One concerns his rejection of the attempt to point to God by discovering "gaps" in our knowledge of the natural order. He read the physicist Von Weisäcker's book, *The History of Nature,* and saw even more clearly what had been happening in the development of modern science. As principles of natural explanation of phenomena are discovered, theologians have tended to look for some special place where God can act directly in his world. But these areas have become more and more restricted as science pushes back into the natural order. Bonhoeffer says Von Weisäcker has brought home to him ". . . how wrong it is to use God as a stop-gap for the incompleteness of our knowledge. . . . We should find God in what we do know, not in what we don't; not in outstanding problems but in those we have already solved."[5]

A further reflection came out of Bonhoeffer's meditation on the meaning of the cross.

Man's religiosity makes him look in his distress to the power of God in the world; he uses God as a *Deus ex machina.* The Bible however directs him to the powerlessness and suffering of God; only a suffering God can help.

And he calls this a clearing of the decks for the God of the Bible who "conquers power and space in the world by his weakness."[6]

In these five themes, so sharply and yet tantalizingly suggested by

Bonhoeffer, we have very nearly the complete summary of the crucial points in the new theological development.

We see theology here requiring of itself a reexamination of the very basis of the possibility of speaking about God and his action in the world. Man "come of age" asks the question about God, when he asks it at all, out of a new understanding of his world.

II

Bonhoeffer's significance as the prophet of the new theological era was realized only slowly. His martyrdom gave the church one of its powerful demonstrations of faith doing its work in love; but his theological ideas, undergoing radical development as they were in the last brief writings, came to their full influence only after his death. In the United States for example it was the generation of college students after the war which first found Bonhoeffer speaking directly to their condition. There have been two main aspects of the new theological context. Both are foreshadowed in Bonhoeffer, but it would be far from the mark to say that he directly created the new tendencies especially in their extreme form. Rather it was he who sensed the areas where the theological problems were now going to be faced. We can look at these two main developments since Bonhoeffer. I will call these the political-ethical area, and the area of questioning about our knowledge of God.

Certainly the movement of modern theology we have called the "renaissance" was highly conscious of the political and moral responsibility of the Christian and of the church in the world. Karl Barth, for all his early emphasis on the futility of human idealism, saw the search for justice in the world as a parable of the Christian's knowledge of the divine justice. The theologies of Reinhold and Richard Niebuhr and of Paul Tillich all gave a strong affirmation of the responsibility of man for justice and a tolerable public order. It is true that these theologians were critical of what they re-

garded as the superficial optimism of the liberal period. They believed that history can be understood only as it stands under the
judgment of the Kingdom of God. They were all anti-Utopians.
Where then has the new social ethical concern made any difference?

The point is perhaps primarily one of emphasis, but the shift
might be described as a return to ethical action in the world as the
center of Christian witness, rather than as an implication of a faith
which transcends purely ethical and this-worldly concerns. In the
early days of the neo-orthodox period H. Richard Niebuhr, Wilhelm Pauck and Francis P. Miller published a book entitled *The
Church Against the World.* This title gives the dominant note of
theology between the world wars. The Church has its unique life
and witness which makes it a center of critical judgment against
the secular order and its ideals, although the church accepts responsibility for culture and the task of political justice.

The mood of the radical political and theological activists after
the second world war is much more that of the worldly Christianity
which sees the church as the community which sends its members
out into the world to work on the frontiers of historical action
where revolutionary reconstruction is called for. It is the isolation
of the church from the central issues of power and social justice
which troubles this new generation. They see Christian responsibility as concrete political action in the realm of racial justice, for
example. In countries in revolutionary ferment such as those in
Africa, in Latin America, and behind the Iron Curtain, the church
finds itself in one sense quite powerless. Yet responsibility for the
Kingdom of God leads to the question, what shall we do within
these movements which are reshaping the world, and which bear
for better or worse, much of the hopes for a new justice and vitality
in society? There are always aspects of political ideologies which the
Christian faith must view with suspicion and even with outright
opposition. Where there is an inhuman and vicious idolatry such as

that in the Nazi movement the only answer is resistance. But in the political and economic ferment today the drive toward new forms of political order is often ambiguously constructive and destructive. Merely to resist is to be irrelevant or to defend the conservative side on every issue.[7]

We shall see some of the specific ethical implications of this concern for political action in the next chapter, but here one important consequence must be noted. Once again the ethical life, that is the life of responsible action in the world and for the neighbor, is taken to be the central theme of theology. The theologies of justification by faith always stressed the transcendence of the ethical in the Christian view of man and God. Sin is estrangement of the spirit. It is manifest in ethical irresponsibility, but its depth can never be put in wholly ethical terms. So the new life in grace is more than the ethically responsible life. But there is in the New Testament the insistence that the test of faith is in action. It is those who have fed the hungry and clothed the naked, and visited those in prison whom the Lord accepts at the Last Judgment as expressed in Matthew's Gospel, and this point asserts itself again and again in the history of the church. The concept of a worldly Christianity is really a reassertion of the ethical witness of the Gospel. It is in action for the neighbor that the real test of the symbols and professions of faith is to be found. This has been clearly put by one of the leaders of the American church in the civil rights movement. Robert Spike makes very clear how the task of theology is felt in the new stress on moral action in the world:

This is where we have failed so miserably in our propositional theology—explaining what ought to happen to individuals and society if they truly followed Christ. Few people get preached into action. It was not until the shadow of turmoil actually touched some white people, in the early 1960's . . . only when they began to break out of the frozen mould of the "way to behave" in demonstrations and political actions—and were jailed, that the theology became clear. There must be a deed before there can be a doctrine that makes any sense.[8]

This ethical theology has a fresh note of optimism about what man can do. This is one of its most striking characteristics. The confidence of modern man that he can meet his problems with his own resources is seen as an aspect of culture which the Christian faith must accept and with which we must live. It will be remembered that Bonhoeffer stressed this self-confidence of modern man, even though he had witnessed the debacle of the Hitler regime.

III

The question which has come to the center of attention in the new phase of twentieth century theology is, "where and how does God make a difference in the world?" If this seems an unusual and even unreligious way to put the question it is the precise way in which it is being put by such men as Bishop Robinson and by a group of theologians who have come to considerable public attention through their position that God indeed does no longer make a difference to man, if he ever did. The appearance of the "theology of the death of God" within the work of Christian theologians has some unusual aspects, to put it mildly. We must try to make some assessment of the significance of this development.

The theme of the "death of God" has created highly charged and emotional public reactions. There are many who sensibly ask how non-belief in God can be called theology at all, let alone Christian theology. It will be well for the present writer to state what his own perspective on the "death of God" movement is, before trying to characterize it.

I regard the so-called "death of God" theologies as the recurrence of very old problems in man's religious quest. The roots of the problem do not lie so much in modern secularism, or man's coming of age, as in the mystery of man's being and the fact that God does not make himself obvious and always present to us. The turn to a wistful or a self-confident humanism has happened many times in human thought, and it is unusual but not impossible to find examples of it in Christian experience long before the present era.

The Psalmist knows the absence of God:

My eyes grow dim with waiting for my God. (Psalm 69:3)

Hide not thy face from thy servant; for I am in distress, make haste to answer me. (Psalm 69:17)

The story of man's life may be understood as man's quest for God and as God's quest for man. God's withdrawing himself may be one side of the history, man's turning away or his hardening of his mind against God may be another. The groping and limitation of man, the struggle with inadequate concepts of God, and sometimes the sheer confusion of tongues and ideas can destroy the realization of God's presence. The history of religions is strewn with images of gods who have, in the myths and stories, died or been slain. Some have suggested that the death of God has a psycho-analytic explanation in the need for the child to move beyond the dominance of the Father. Man's coming of age may be deeply involved in the need to assert his freedom against God. He can easily confuse this with a denial or disappearance of God.

Unquestionably there is something in the modern spirit which has intensified man's sense of being free from God. Friedrich Nietzsche gave a kind of proto-prophecy of the present movement in his *Thus Spake Zarathrustra* when he proclaimed the murder of God by man.[9] Much of modern existentialism is radically atheistic, although the father of existentialism, Sören Kierkegaard said "It is the God-relationship which makes a man a man." [10] What Martin Buber has called the "Eclipse of God" is a pervasive aspect of modern culture.[11] It should not be exaggerated. The thesis that urban, sophisticated, secularized man has no sense of religious need or concern is an easy generalization only partly supportable. Bonhoeffer did see however that there is a new turn in man's experience when he begins to look at his problems wholly without reference to God as traditionally conceived.

It is not therefore merely the sense that God is absent, or the wistfulness of a concern about where to find him which marks the radical movement toward a theology without God. What is distinctive of this movement is its announcement that the Christian faith, the Christian way of life, full Christian existence can and must now be expressed in a world where God either simply is not there for us, or where indeed in some mystical sense he once was but now has died. I should agree with those who allow the name of theology for this new tendency; partly because it arises in the Christian community and offers itself as an interpretation of Christian faith; and partly because its existential concern is, like that of all theology, centered upon the nature of fulfillment and truth in human existence. It has a passion for the theological question about God even though its answer is hardly distinguishable from any other atheism. The moral passion in the "death of God" thinkers is bound up with the new secularism and the search for a worldly Christianity. The three themes appear to be: man does not need God, man is set free by the death of God as an historical event, and man cannot know God anyhow because his knowledge is restricted to what he can know scientifically and God is not discovered in experience. These three themes are worked out by the best known leaders of this group, William Hamilton, Thomas Altizer and Paul Van Buren. We can look at each in turn.

Perhaps the soberest and best general account of the movement by one of its representatives is that by William Hamilton in an article "The Death of God Theology" published in the *Christian Scholar* in the spring of 1965. Hamilton keeps a somewhat ambiguous openness on the question of whether there really is a God in this article. His main theme is that God solves no problems and meets no needs.

> We concentrate our energy and passion on the specific, the concrete, the personal. We turn from the problems of faith to the reality of love. We walk away from the inner anguish of a Hamlet or an Oedipus and take up our worldly responsibility with Prospero and Orestes. As Protestants, we push the movement from church to world as far as it can go and become frankly worldly men. And in this world, as we have seen, there is no need for religions and no need for God.[12]

Later in the same year Hamilton wrote an autobiographical piece in which the theme of waiting for God which appears in the previous article seems to be set aside for a more explicit assertion that we must really speak of the death of God for it means a "real loss, something irretrievable." He still keeps his description of Christian stance as loyalty to Jesus because Jesus "is the one to whom I repair, the one before whom I stand, the one whose way with others is also to be my way because there is something there in his words, his life, his way with others, his death, that I do not find elsewhere." [13]

Thomas Altizer's doctrine is rooted in a mystical approach to religious experience, especially as this involves the tension, oppositions and dialectic of the sacred and the profane. Here again the theme of worldly Christianity becomes the key. The way to the assertion of man's maturity and his creativity is his willingness to accept the profane and to change it. The collapse of the transcendence of Being, that is the death of God, can be the "liberation of man." This event is the Creative Word by which man lives, and that word is present in Jesus, standing in history and disclosing the possibility of man's transendence of history. Altizer's view is quite Nietzschean, only now it is Jesus and not the prophet of the superman who gives humanity its liberation.[14]

Paul Van Buren's book, *The Secular Meaning of the Gospel,* also announces a Christianity without God, but one which is centered in Jesus and the Easter Event, since Jesus is the man for others who discloses true freedom. Van Buren makes use of two types of analysis of the problem of truth in modern linguistic philosophy. One is the verification principle which restricts meaning to assertions which can be confirmed by direct observation, usually confined to sense data. The other is the analysis of the use of language in its various contexts so that its meaning is disclosed in its function of clarifying some human attitude or action. Van Buren mixes these two principles in a way which I find confusing, but the upshot for him is clear. It is that the word "God" is meaningless because it cannot refer to anything verifiable, and the word "God" is dead because it has no significant use for secular man. Therefore, Christianity is a faith and a way of understanding life based on the life of Jesus and the experience of liberation which the New Testament speaks of as the Resurrection.[15]

It is curious that Van Buren and other logical empiricists take no account of the work of the empirical theologians such as Douglas Clyde Macintosh, and Henry Nelson Wieman, who adopted the empirical method as the way to theological knowledge and held that the immanent God can be known by critical rational interpretation of what we experience. One reason that the empirical argument in theology has been neglected by the new school would appear to be the long dominance of the theologies of revelation. It is noteworthy that the more recent discussion of the limits of knowledge in the linguistic school have been less dogmatic about the possibility of knowing some metaphysical aspects of reality than Van Buren is.[16] These issues illustrate our opening remark, that the problems of the knowledge of God are perennial problems for human reflection, not just curiosities of the twentieth century. The positivist thesis which convinces Van Buren that there is no possible knowledge of God is as old as Protagoras, 450 B.C.

Many who have sympathy with Van Buren's interpretation of the present state of "empirically minded man" yet would not go so far as he does in saying that this eliminates the possibility of speaking of God altogether. There are some who are more interested in the sociological aspect of modern man's empiricism. They see in man's new secularized urbanized existence with its technical proficiency and possibilities the key to the difficulty of traditional ways of speaking about God. This thesis is found in Harvey Cox's *The Secular City* and in **Gabriel** Vahanian's *The Death of God*. These social theorists argue that contemporary man has a new form of human existence. He is learning to meet his problems without specifically "religious" resources. Metaphysical ways of thinking, that is, concerns about ultimate causes, goals, and principles are irrelevant in this new style of life. Therefore theology which tries to speak intelligibly about God's being represents a vestigial remnant of bourgeois mentality. This sociological thesis on the disappearance of metaphysics received its classic statement in the thought of August Compte at the end of the eighteenth century. It was the Comptian spirit which enthroned the Goddess of Reason in the revolution. Something akin to this seems implied in the present theme of the disappearance of the old ways of speaking about God, though Christian interpreters like Harvey Cox and Vahanian believe that God is not "dead," and that new ways of encountering his presence and power will be disclosed in the new order.

No one can look at the history of Christian thought about God, and its counterparts in all of man's religious and philosophical quest without recognizing that there is much unfinished business here for the human mind and spirit. Whitehead says the progress of religion is defined by the denunciation of gods. When it is announced that God is dead we have the right to ask whether it is not some human misunderstanding or distortion or complacency about God which has been exposed. Very often when men have shifted from one metaphysical outlook to another this has been proclaimed as the end of metaphysics whereas it is really the emergence of a new set of categories for speaking about our existence.

It appears that the revolt against what is taken to be the meaning of the tradition has all but made it impossible for these thinkers to consider possible alternative interpretations of the concept of God and his action in the world. Also, how any sense is to be made of the New Testament picture of Jesus apart from his continually uttered and enacted relationship to God the Father is not by any means clear. The claim that this group draws inspiration from the later Bonhoeffer must be accepted as an accurate statement for those who make it; but Bonhoeffer never proclaimed a Christianity without God; he called for a Christianity which does not depend on God to do things which man himself can and ought to do. That is a very different matter.[17]

IV

We have said that this new context of theological discussion is not discontinuous with the issues and problems which have informed theology for the past four centuries, and the opening decades of the twentieth century. The issues for theology are still those which arise from the search for the relation of theological truth to the truth which man has through science and reason and experience. The concern for understanding the nature of man and the reality of the new life which is made possible when man is released from

bondage to illusion and self-centeredness is still the center of the
discussion. How is God known and where is his grace experienced?
There are two lines of response to the present theological questioning which have presented alternatives both to traditional theology
and to some of the major theological constructions in the first part
of the twentieth century. I shall call the first the way of the new
personalism, and the second the way of the new metaphysics of
process. These are modes of theological thought rather than finished
systems. We can ask how they propose to interpret theological language in the light of the problems which Bonhoeffer and those
who come after him have raised.

Radical personalism is the position that knowledge of God and
language about God is possible only in the situation of direct personal confession and communication. For this view the truth with
which Christianity is concerned is not available in the form of sub-
jective structures, or fixed doctrines. Neither is it available in the
form of biblical exegesis when that is undertaken as an objective
exercise in interpretation. It is only when the truth of the biblical
witness becomes personal truth for the one who speaks and the one
who hears that God can be known.

We have already noted this position in the religious philosophy
of Martin Buber. Emil Brunner based his entire theological construction upon this conception of personal truth. What we find in
theology since Bonhoeffer is this position even more radically
stated. It takes the form of both a theological method and a method
of biblical interpretation.

The radical nature of the position is manifest in Helmut Gollwitzer's book *The Existence of God as Confessed by Faith*. For
Gollwitzer all "objectifying" in theological thought is inappro-
priate, unbiblical and futile in the quest for Christian truth. Certainly God is objective to us. Gollwitzer wants to keep this aspect
of Christian faith. God is not a projection of our minds. But knowl-

edge of God is possible only in the confessional and communicative situation.

> The Old and New Testament writers . . . speak of God with the most massive objectivity, yet in such a way that they stringently avoid objectifying talk as being inappropriate to *this* object because generalizing it and keeping it at an examinable distance.[18]

We cannot therefore examine what we say about God as we analyze what we say about the world. Yet we do speak about him. We speak of his power, his majesty, his love. We have to understand all expressions about God's nature as interpretations of personal communication or revelation.

> 'Attributes of God' are not descriptions of an entity that are made in quiet observation, but accounts of what is revealed in the self-manifestation of God that takes place in God's address and action. . . . Revelation of God is manifestation of his will, and living inauguration of communion.[19]

Thus the speech of personal communion replaces all structural concepts. There is no ontology of God, that is, no doctrine of his being. There is only the speech in which his being is present as personal self-disclosure.

We find here the doctrine that being is known through the act of speech, and this means both the being of God and human being. Gollwitzer finds much of his inspiration for this view in the work of Rosenstock-Huessy who says that "God, world, man are vocatives, not nominatives" which is Huessy's way of saying what is meant when some say properly speaking God cannot be expressed but only addressed.[20]

It is however in the later philosophy of Heidegger that the doc-

trine of language as disclosure of being has received its most trench-
ant statement. Many European theologians have adopted this
Heideggerian view, as in the work of Heinrich Ott. This is an interesting example of how philosophy as a route to knowledge of being
which has been put out the front door of theology returns by another entrance, in this case the philosophy of language. The development is clear in the work of the post-Bultmannians. Ernst Fuchs
for example says:

> Language makes being itself into an event. . . . The language
> of faith brings into language the gathering of faith and thereby
> Christ. It admits Christ into that existence which we ourselves
> enter upon in the name of Jesus.[21]

Professor James Robinson has done important work in interpreting this movement in his book *A New Quest of the Historical Jesus*
and in his essay in the volume entitled *The New Hermeneutic*
which he has edited with John Cobb, Jr.[22] He gives a careful review
of the position as developed by Fuchs, Gadamer, and Ebeling. Its
crux is the virtual identification of systematic theology with biblical
interpretation (hermeneutic) through the use of the concept of the
word-event. The task of theology is so to interpret biblical language
that the way is opened to personal communication. "Thus the object of dogmatic theology is the word-event itself, in which the
reality of man comes true." [23] We note especially the tense of the
verb here. The truth in theology and biblical interpretation is a
happening. The word becomes true in the event of being spoken
and heard so that faith is created and is present.

The impressiveness of this position is constituted in part by the
obvious care with which it seeks to do justice to the nature of faith,
and its rejection of a naive speech about God which treats him as
just another object of knowledge. But its power appears also in that

it seems to be a way of avoiding many difficult problems about the relation of God to the world. It seems to bypass the issue of how contemporary man's understanding of his world is compatible with the world-view of Scripture. If the truth can only be known in personal communication, then there are no criteria outside our speech about God by which the sense or nonsense of what we say may be judged. Thus the position appears at first glance to solve the questions raised by modern science, philosophy and metaphysics concerning the tests of truth so far as theology is concerned. If theological language is self-contained, self-judging, and has its meaning only as it is being spoken and heard in faith it is impregnable.

As we turn to the second type of contemporary reconstruction, the process theology, we find theologians who believe that this "impregnability" of theological language is gained at too great a cost. It leaves no way of relating Christian faith positively to the thought-world of modern man. The alternative as seen by the process thinkers is to continue the metaphysical task of developing a rational view of the world in which the forms of nature and human existence are understood in a positive relationship to the creative being of God who is himself both process and structure. We have taken note of the process theologies in the previous chapter. Here we may characterize briefly the way in which this position deals with the problems which concern the new personalists.

First, process theologians all agree that the categories for understanding reality must include the dynamic and personal aspect of reality. It is a defect of the Platonic and Kantian traditions that they treat abstract structures as more fundamental than creative process. Following Whitehead and Hartshorne, process theologians hold that all structure is abstraction from concrete reality which is creative process. God's being should not be identified with pure form, or with an impassive absolute in which time disappears. He is the creative spirit at work in time. His being includes formal structure for he gives intelligibility and order to the world, but he is more than logical structure. Process theologians regard the new personalism as in its own way an extreme reaction to the static view of God. They welcome the correction but believe there is no reason for surrendering the objectivity of metaphysical inquiry. What we need is a metaphysics which includes time and personal existence in the structure of being and which can illuminate aspects of the Christian apprehension of reality. One possible way of interpreting the present discussion is to say that the new personalists are really developing a metaphysical position based on personal action and communication, only they do not choose to call it metaphysics.

As to language, process theology interprets language as do the personalists, as functioning within the context of personal life and communication. Meanings cannot be ripped out of their setting in history. All speech about ultimate matters involves our faith and our personal valuation. The American pragmatists emphasized this truth about language before the existentialists did. But here again, to say that the act of speaking and hearing itself constitutes being, as the personalists do, seems to simplify and distort the relation of language to reality. We all know what it means to grope for the right word when we try to express something deeply felt, but for which no words seem adequate. Man is more than speaking and hearing. He is living spirit, expressed in a physical organism, and participating in the life of a world which is more than all our symbols for speaking about it. Whitehead says that no form of words is ever the adequate expression of a proposition.[24] The meaning of a proposition must be felt, and it leads us to seek for its adequate analysis and articulation.

A third point is made not only by process theologians but many others who see in the new personalism a parochial point of view of the relation of Christianity to other faiths, which make it difficult to conceive of any significant discussion beyond the boundaries of the Christian community. The new hermeneutics seems so focused upon biblical interpretation alone that it tends to ignore all questions about the relation of Christianity to culture. On the question of the nature of faith, Gerhard Ebeling for example says:

> Only the relation to the true, the living God, can be faith. The relationship with other gods by its very nature cannot be called faith at all.
>
> The Christian faith is true faith, simply faith, just as Christian love is not a special kind of love, but true love, simply love.
>
> When the Easter faith comes into being, what is new is not a new object of faith, but the coming into being, the being awakened and coming alive of faith itself.[25]

This seems to relegate everything in man's experience outside Christianity to an inferior if not irrelevant status. Thus the new hermeneutical position continues the exclusiveness of the theological method which Karl Barth has inaugurated.

Process theologians believe that there is an alternative to this narrowness in the new personalism. They agree with Ian Ramsey, who has analyzed the problem of religious knowledge from a somewhat different point of view, that the Christian knowledge of God has analogues in our knowledge of the world and of other persons.[26] The task is to see how the Biblical faith is to be interpreted in relation to the kinds of experience which contemporary man has of his world, and to the evolutionary historical picture of the life of nature and of human existence. Process theologians are not at all concerned to get rid of natural theology, but believe that only in relation to a more adequate scientific, philosophical and theological understanding of nature can the contemporary man's questions about God be given meaningful answers. John Cobb Jr.'s book, *A Christian Natural Theology,* is one example of the way in which process theology interprets the doctrine of God in relation to the scientific picture of the world.

This interest in a theology which brings the dimension of historical and natural process into the very meaning of God's being is by no means confined to the group we have called process theologians because of their primary indebtedness to Alfred North Whitehead. Three Roman Catholic thinkers may be mentioned as outstanding interpreters of a similar point of view within the Catholic framework. The most widely known is Teilhard de Chardin who in his *The Phenomenon of Man*, and *The Divine Milieu* and many other works develops his vision of evolutionary process which makes contact with scientific knowledge and which expresses a mystical religious view of the whole. It remains to be seen, in the judgment of the present writer, whether de Chardin's work can be said to be established on a critical scientific foundation. As an imaginative vision of the world in the light of time and evolution it is unquestionably exciting and provocative. A French Catholic, Claude Tresmontant is developing a biblical theology under the inspiration of Bergson's version of process metaphysics.[27] He criticizes the theological tradition with its separation of God from time and process. The Dutch Jesuit, Peter Schoonenberg, who finds important suggestions in de Chardin, has given a sober and critical evolutionary theology in his book, *God's World in the Making*. Schoonenberg relates the history of salvation as biblically understood to the scientific study of the development of man through the stages of the anonymous beginning, the religious self-expression, clarity in Israel, and the fulness of Christ. He goes on to consider ethical issues in the new outlook in connection with marriage and work. He sees that in the Christian view salvation should more and more transform labor, though we should not develop a one-sided mystique of labor in a "lyric consecration of the world." But the resurrection of the Lord "who labored in the human vineyard and worked for our salvation can project its light on the world of labor."[28]

Theology seems split between the extremes of a personalism exclusively concentrated on the Christian faith viewed from within, and a theology which sees the Christian faith as a perspective on man's religious quest which must be expressed with a continuing metaphysical insight into the nature of the world and of all human experience. Yet we see that both are breaking out of traditional patterns, and it may be that the spirit of their search for a living, personal fulfillment of man's life with God has a deeper unity than appears in these disparate types of theological thought.

CHAPTER IV

Christian Ethics and Society

IF ONE clear straight line could be drawn from the Gospel to Christianity's moral standard for society Christian history would have been quite different. Either the Christian ethic would have been abandoned somewhere along the way as impossible, or the church would have neatly separated those who conformed to the standard in idea and practice from those who did not. We would know exactly what a Christian society is. But there is no such straight line. Nothing in Jesus' teaching, or in the Bible taken as a whole, or in all the centuries of Christian experience gives us a standard pattern of what society should be, or one simple answer as to what Christians should do about the political, economic and other choices they have to make. Churches and church members are always to be found supporting conflicting political and social movements.

Perhaps there are several "ideas of a Christian society," to use Mr. T. S. Eliot's phrase; or perhaps there is no such thing. The Gospel gives us ultimate principles often expressed in cryptic sayings: "If a man asks for your cloak, give him your coat also"; "render unto Caesar the things that are Caesar's and unto God the things that are God's"; "Love your neighbor as yourself." But when we try to use these principles in specific judgments about such problems as economic justice or the moral significance of the use of atomic weapons, we have many perplexities. The more we analyze the moral choices we have to make, the more we come to see that underlying every Christian ethic there is a judgment as to the meaning and nature of the Gospel. Has Christ given us a new law by which to live, and thus made it possible for us to draw an outline of the Christian way of life? Or has the revelation in Christ disclosed a spirit of love which is free from the law, and yet responsible, so that we must undertake to make decisions without the guidance of a specific pattern of Christian life? We see why ethical questions are also theological questions for the Christian. Ultimate beliefs about God and human life are involved.

In this chapter we shall characterize five major traditions of Christian ethics. These are the Roman Catholic, Anglican, Lutheran, liberal Protestant, and Calvinist-Puritan traditions. Of course these are streams which have flowed into one another in history. We shall examine the types of ethics from two main points of view. First, it is possible to trace a certain convergence toward a common Christian understanding of the problem of ethics today in the search for the basis of a peaceful, decent, and tolerable social order. Second, we must formulate some of the important issues which are being discussed today not only between Roman Catholic and Protestant ethics, but also within types of Protestant ethics.

The basis for this convergence of ethical judgment is that there is on all sides a deeper recognition of the significance of the two complementary principles which follow directly from the attempt to see human life in the light of Christ. These principles are not legalistic rules; they are essential guides to the Christian understanding of what man is. One is the personal principle. This means the supreme evaluation which Christian faith puts upon personal existence. Every person is created for a life of dignity and fellowship in the grace of God's eternal purpose. It is how God sees each man, not how other men see him, which confers upon the person his essential right to a free and responsible life, serving God with that unique and irreplaceable quality which belongs to each one.

The social principle means that persons are created "members one of another" as the New Testament says. We exist in a social relationship with God, our creator; and we are created for and in a community of life with one another. It is especially important to see that these two principles, the personal and the social, belong absolutely together. We could even say that each is only a full statement of what is implied in the other. For the Christian faith, no one can realize his personal worth except as an interdependent member of the community of persons. We realize our own freedom in giving and receiving from others. On the other hand, all human society is made up of free, unique selves, each of which potentially has something to give to the whole which no other can give. We can underline the importance of these two principles taken together by recalling how fundamental in all Christian thought is the pattern of the family. Our deepest insight into the nature of God is expressed with a family analogy. He is both Father and Son bound together in one Spirit. We are created to be brothers under God, the Father. The human family is our best illustration of how each person grows in his unique potentialities by sharing in the loving care of a society of other persons. Yet each member of the family discovers what it is to give of himself for the sake of the others. The human family is only an analogy both for our thought about God and about society; but no Christian thought gets very far away from it.

While there is then no one Christian social philosophy, we can say that no philosophy which does not do justice to the personal and the social principles can be accepted by Christians. This means that Christian appraisals of society will always search out and stand against violations of either principle. The late Nicolas Berdyaev was one of the most powerful Christian critics of modern societies, because he so unfailingly exposed the way in which ruthless political powers, impersonal standards of money and prestige, and the imposition of authoritarian ethical standards are all sources of modern bondage. In his *Slavery and Freedom* Berdyaev showed how a sheer individualism and an extreme collectivism alike thwart the person in his freedom and his essential community with others. "One sets an abstraction, 'society,' above the person. The other sets an abstraction, the 'individual,' above the society of persons." In the ruthless exploitation of totalitarian regimes or the use of men as means to the ends of market and profit, we find some of the greatest threats to the Christian goal of the free person in the community of other persons.

Contemporary Christian ethics generally exhibits a realistic acknowledgment of the involvement of all human institutions in evils which are not to be removed simply through more strenuous moral effort. Yet this acknowledgment does not eliminate the importance of the choices which men and nations make. Indeed in an increasingly complex and interdependent society the decisions of leaders and citizens have the most fateful consequences history has ever known. The Christian concern for human life, for freedom of the spirit, and for justice requires an effective strategy for controlling the ruthless abuse of power. Decisions have to be made which involve the search for a social policy which offers some hope for peace and orderly human relationships.

An important indication of the climate of theological opinion in which such discussions go on in the church today is afforded by the attempts of the two meetings of the World Council of Churches, the first at Amsterdam in 1948 and the second at Evanston in 1954, to grapple with the question of the Christian attitude toward the clash of nations and economic systems. The Amsterdam conference arrived at a statement concerning capitalism and communism which created widespread discussion. The statement said, "The Christian churches should reject the ideologies of both communism and *laissez-faire* capitalism, and should seek to draw men away from the false assumption that these extremes are the only alternatives."[1]

The discussion at the Evanston Assembly six years later reflected the awareness that such a general disavowal, while intelligible as an attempt to assert the freedom of Christian judgment from identification with any particular social program or ideology, still had a certain abstract and unreal character about it. The issues in the world today have to do with the political embodiments of Marxist, socialist, and modified capitalist programs amidst vast social upheaval. A Preparatory Commission noted that "there is little support in countries with a democratic tradition either for consistent collectivism or a purely *laissez-faire* economy."[2] The Conference report said that the development of "a common ethos and common convictions concerning the destiny of man and his relation to society" is a task set before the churches. It is interesting to observe that by far the fullest and best account of the development of the social ethical discussion in the World Council of Churches has been written by a Roman Catholic, Edward Duff, S.J. Writing with sympathy and objectivity he points out the difficulties of arriving at a common mind among the churches on the nature of Christian ethics itself in relation to the Christian faith.[3] We need to see why different positions about the place of ethics in the Christian life are taken, and how they lead to different ethical judgments on specific issues. We shall begin with Roman Catholic thought.

I

Generalizations about the social policy and ethical outlook of the Roman Catholic Church could be made with a fair degree of confidence during the years from the Council of Trent to the Second Vatican Council. Certainly there were many internal struggles, but the dogmatic authority of the Church seemed to hold a consistent line on traditional positions regarding church and state, the implications of natural law for the family and economic life, and all realms of cultural value. To those outside, the Roman Church presented something very like a monolithic structure.

The "up-dating" of the Church's position on theological and ethical issues and on the form and practice of the church called for by Pope John and achieved by the Council is so extraordinary that it is difficult to give a significant characterization of the Roman Church's position today without an extended analysis of the background and results of the work of Vatican II. That cannot be attempted here, but we can recognize that what has been done by the Council was the result of a long period of quiet constructive thought which opened the way to the new era. We can note some of the most important aspects of this history. We see that the task of balancing the personal and social principles has been undertaken with a deepening sense of the significance of personal freedom, and the necessity for putting restrictions upon ecclesiastical power. The task is to create structures of social justice which assert and protect the claims of those who have the least power to make demands upon the social body.

Catholic social thought has its modern charter in many Papal Encyclicals beginning with *Rerum Novarum* in 1891 and coming down to *Quadragesimo Anno* in 1931, and *Pacem in Terris* in 1963. Here the Church seeks a "middle way" between unrestrained capitalism and totalitarian socialism. The rights of private property are upheld. So also are the rights of workers' organizations. Conditions in the economic world which drive men to ruthless exploitation and which put them under conditions of poverty to drain out the energies of the spirit are condemned. What the encyclicals propose, to be sure with great caution and moderation, has been taken up as a program of Catholic action toward liberal democracy by prophetic spirits like Dom Luigi Sturzo. Lay people and priests close to the common people are often found giving expression to a groundswell of democratic sentiment looking toward a revision of structures of unequal privilege and power.

In the United States today we may point to the brilliantly edited liberal Catholic *Commonweal,* and to the Catholic labor paper, *Work,* published in Chicago, as leading voices for social reconstruction. Miss Barbara Ward, British Catholic, is one of the best-informed Christian interpreters of economic problems. She brings an acute ethical judgment to bear on the problem of finding a democratic alternative to communism.[4] The point here is not to set up the ideal of democracy as the test for progressive Christian thought, and then to approve when Catholics or others measure up to it. The point is that all sensitive Christian thought today must define the personal and social principles so that the Christian evaluation of life becomes a prophetic criticism against the evils of present society, and a light to point the way to a better order. There is a growing edge of Roman Catholic thought which recognizes that no single past system will do, and which is seeking to quicken the conscience of the Church to constructive action in the present world-wide crisis.

That part of Roman ethical theory which is most readily intelligible to non-Catholics is the conception of natural law. The Roman Church rests great weight on this doctrine, for here in principle it has a basis for ethical judgment which is accessible to all men. Natural law consists of the truths about man's obligations which follow from the structure of human existence and which therefore reason can discover and define with some adequacy. Catholic legal theory, for example, rests upon the doctrine that behind positive law there is the universal and unwritten natural law. Of course in practice it is the Church which finally decides what the natural law is.

We shall note Protestant criticism of this natural law theory in a moment. But it is important to recognize that much depends on the content which is put into the natural law. Actually the concept can be looked at as an empty vessel which is filled with new content as ethical sensitivity enlarges. The increasing emphasis in Catholic theory on the "common good" as the standard of political rights and responsibilities is worked out within the framework of natural law theory by Jacques Maritain. For example, Maritain includes within his scheme of human rights those of "free investigation and discussion," "the right of every citizen to participate actively in political life," "equal suffrage for all," "the right to a just wage," and the right "freely to form vocational groups or trade unions."[5] This represents a considerable influence of the modern democratic conscience on the way in which human rights are understood.

Such a description of rights introduces into "natural law" concepts which may be ambiguous and which certainly are debatable. This difficulty appears when the positive law and the law of nations seek to give more objective and legally enforceable status to specific principles. One Protestant criticism of natural law theory is that the Church not only puts its authority behind the ultimate principles, but it treats very complicated and debatable deductions from these principles as if they had the same authority. Maritain admits that there are "imperceptible transitions" from natural law principles to consequences in positive laws. It is just the "imperceptibility" of these transitions which makes them suspicious. This is the real theological point of the familiar criticism of Catholic ethics concerning medical practice, planned parenthood, and similar issues. Deciding what is natural is a naturally difficult question!

A second Protestant criticism of the natural law concept is that it puts a legalistic restriction upon the freedom of the Christian conscience in dealing with the unpredictable and always problematical stuff of actual social existence. Natural law theory is so completely integrated into the Catholic structure that it is hardly conceivable that there could be a Catholic ethics which would totally reject it. But many Catholic moralists see difficulty in handling ethical problems solely within the traditional natural law doctrines. They show increasing flexibility in trying to relate Christian ethics to concrete circumstances. An illustration is the case of modern warfare. Catholic theory in the past has dealt with the moral problem involved in war by a theory of the "just war," and by the application of an explicit humane code of ethics to nations which wage war. But in technological warfare in which the very weapons often make impossible discrimination between combatants and noncombatants, where the whole productive capacity and citizenry of a nation makes up the war potential, the chivalrous formulas of the past become almost irrelevant. All Christian moral theory is in travail over this problem. One Catholic legal theorist heard by the writer confessed frankly the great difficulty of making past definitions of natural law ethics adequate to cope with the issues involved in modern war. One further word must be said here in fairness to the Catholic position. Whereas Protestant ethics has traditionally rejected the theory of natural law, it has had its own parallel in the idea of the "orders" of creation such as family and state, which are given by God and in their own structure show something of what is expected of man as he serves God in this kind of world. All Christian ethics must find some pattern in experience and reason for the explicit guidance of life. Love is greater than any law or principle; but it cannot work responsibly without the aid of principles.

The Roman Catholic theory of the relation of church and state has been a point of major tension with Protestant critics. James Hastings Nichols' *Democracy and the Churches,* Anson Phelps Stokes' *Church and State in the United States,* and John Bennett's *Christianity and the State* give Protestant perspectives. But the Second Vatican Council has made a clear declaration for complete religious liberty. The movement in this direction had its courageous pioneers such as Father John Courtney Murray, the American Jesuit, who was intimately involved in the new declaration. Murray published in 1949 an essay entitled "Contemporary Orientations of Catholic Thought on Church and State in the Light of History." [6] He saw that the Roman Church was tending toward a redefinition of the relation of the spiritual and temporal powers. This has come about in the light of modern democracy which represents not only a new fact to which all churches must adjust, but a principle which is "natural" and which expresses a tendency of history which must be accepted as having its rational and moral justification. Murray wants to formulate the "primacy of the spiritual power" in a way which will make more clear "the primacy of the spiritual." This means that the temporal power, that is society organized politically, has its own sphere and its divine justification directly from God and not from the church. The church, therefore, must deal with the temporal power not in the pattern of state and church as a "dyarchy" of two powers in tension; but rather with the Christian citizen as the locus in which the two powers become an integrity. Therefore, Catholicism is not bound to the theory of the Confessional State which establishes and gives special privilege to one religion. The political freedoms and rights which are important to the Catholic are contained in the very concept of the freedom of the citizen. Such rights, therefore, belong to all citizens equally whatever their religious profession. In harmony with Murray, Maritain also sharply criticizes the attempt at a "pharisaically Christian state" and argues for pluralistic society in which no citizen is put at any disadvantage because he professes or does not profess any specific form of religious faith. [7]

The heart of the new declaration is the following as found in the Schema approved on December 7, 1965:

This Vatican Council declares that the human person has a right to religious freedom. This freedom means that all men are to be immune from coercion on the part of individuals or of social groups and of any human power in such wise that no one is to be forced to act in a manner contrary to his own beliefs whether privately or publicly, whether alone or in association with others, within due limits . . . . . .

This right of the human person to be free is to be recognized in the constitutional law whereby society is governed and this right is to become a civil right. (Sec. II.)

The freedom or immunity from coercion in matters religious which is the endowment of persons as individuals is also to be recognized as their right when they act in community. (Sec. IV.)

II

Anglicanism has an honored tradition of Christian social philosophy which continues to produce prophetic leadership in the church. Frederick Maurice, Charles Gore and William Temple are three of the outstanding figures in the growth of this thought. Temple's clear statement, *Christianity and Social Order*, written for the general reader, gives a convincing summary of a Christian approach to the problem of social justice. Leaders of Anglo-Catholic thought like William Peck, V. A. Demant and Maurice Reckitt have worked continuously at developing principles for the Christian interpretation of man in society. The key theological principle of the whole movement is this: the doctrine of the incarnation is made the basis of all Christian evaluation of culture and political order. In Jesus Christ divine and human natures are united in one person. Here Christianity derives its personal principle. God has made human life the bearer of his own incarnate word. But this is also the source of the social principle, for Christ represents man before God and incorporates us into a new society of which he is the Head. Human society can be interpreted on the analogy of an organism. Our human existence unites personality and community. Therefore, all the positive values of human culture are both derived from the incarnational principle and judged by it. Art, philosophy, the political order are all potential values to be incorporated within the new life in Christ. As the Incarnate Lord, he sums up within his own being the meaning of the whole creation.

The incarnation must be understood in the light of the Cross, the Atonement and the Resurrection. All human values are brought face to face with the perfect love which judges, forgives and redeems. Christ's redemptive action transmutes all the partial values of temporal existence by bringing them within a new order of life whose principle is God's love revealed in all its inclusiveness and its depth.

It is by keeping the personal act of God in the Incarnation at the center of all Christian philosophy that Anglicanism tends to preserve a greater flexibility in its working out of a rational ethics than does most Roman Catholic thought. Also, of course, Anglicans do not labor under the burden of a doctrine of infallibility. Christ's leadership of the Church means the spiritual presence of the Son of God, not the oracular deliverance of dogmatic propositions. We saw in the previous chapter how Anglican theology always seeks a synthesis of faith and reason which leaves each open to the dynamic influence of the other. The Logos incarnate in Christ fulfills and incorporates the highest human reason, but at the same time it transcends all human reason. We cannot by our own power reach high enough to meet God in his ultimate truth. His word reaches down to us.

No single Christian social philosophy can be deduced from this Anglican standpoint with its dynamic and continual synthesis of faith and human thought. Anglican moralists lay special emphasis on the necessity of scientific economics and sociology to provide the data upon which specific Christian judgments are based. But

Christian thought has its own evaluation of economic and sociological findings for human lives are involved, and Christianity has its own way of estimating the worth and progress of human relationships. The over-all direction of Anglican social thought is toward a society which combines personal freedom with responsible sharing in the organic life of the community. Totalitarian claims of either state or church are rejected; but extreme individualism is also rejected. God has created men in an interdependent web of social relationships. Thus this Anglican movement has on the whole reinforced the attempt to find collective solutions to problems of security, health, conditions of labor, and participation of all in the decisions of industry or government. We may appreciate something of the theological integrity and profundity of this school by noting how the doctrine of the Trinity is brought into a new relevance to social problems. God himself incorporates the personal and social principles in his own being. While neither social nor organic analogies adequately describe the Divine Society of Father, Son and Holy Spirit, both analogies are relevant. They remind us that the love which creates us has its origin in a divine life which bears in its own infinite depth the mystery of giving and receiving.

III

We can distinguish three main schools of Protestant social ethics, Lutheran, Liberal and Calvinist-Puritan. The radical thought of the Left Wing Sectarians of the Reformation which was so important in the origins of modern democracy has had its influence upon later times mainly through the other traditions, hence we will not treat it separately here. We shall pursue our thesis that there is a convergence of Christian thought on social ethics today by showing that within each of these three traditions there is a movement toward the others, so that all of them can be seen working toward a new perspective on social problems. Again the central theme is the vision of a society in which personal existence in freedom and dignity is realized in and through participation in the community of men under the judgment and the creative mercy of God.

Traditionally, the Lutheran theory of the Christian relationship to the state and other social orders is characterized by a sharp separation between the realm of society under the law and the spiritual realm of the Christian believers under grace. It is just this separation which has brought the gravest criticism against the Lutheran tradition. Today there is criticism of it from within Lutheranism also. It is important to understand what this doctrine of the "two realms" means. In civil society the Christian has to act according to the law of the state and the rational principles of human justice and equity. God has ordered this realm both as a protection of men against their own sinful tendencies and as a means to the growth of human society. The principles which govern man in society must include therefore the restraint of power, the use of the sword by the state against evildoers within and attack from without. As a believer, living in the fellowship of the Church, the Christian lives in the realm of grace. Here he is governed by the spirit of love which is no law at all, but a free and fully personal relationship between himself and his brothers. It is true this inword spirit will express itself in outward acts. The Christian ruler and the Christian citizen will behave in some respects differently from the non-Christian. But as ruler or citizen he must carry out the inescapable requirements of civil society with its harsh legal necessities of restraint and requital.

Critical estimates of the relation of this "two Kingdom" theory to Luther's own thought differ. In whatever form Luther may have held it, we still recognize that it arises from a realistic perception of the gulf between the fellowship which love seeks and what we actually do to one another in the world. Political action with its compromises, or the destruction and killing in war, can instruct us in what Luther meant by speaking of love's "strange work." Now while the theory of two Kingdoms arises from the tension between the Christian conscience and human action it can also lead to complacency if it is assumed that the Christian remains passive with respect to the deeds and principles of civil society. This may have been the historical effect of the doctrine in leading to a certain passivity of Lutheranism with respect to creative Christian action in society.

It is therefore of great significance that within Lutheranism itself there is a growing criticism of any such outcome in the Christian attitude toward the state. The question was raised most sharply with the Nazi seizure of the German state. "The powers that be are ordained of God," St. Paul says. But suppose groups have seized control by sheer force and wield their power without regard for any standards of political justice or human rights. Suppose the relatively just state turns into the flagrantly unjust state. What then is the Christian to do? In his review of theological thought on the continent of Europe during the Hitler period Dr. W. A. Visser 't Hooft shows how some new ground has been broken on this issue by Lutherans and others.[8] The theology of European Protestantism tends, as we have seen, to be highly concentrated on the Biblical record itself. What does the Bible say about the Christian attitude toward the state? Here the researches of Oscar Cullmann summarized in his *Christ and Time* are typical of the movement toward a new theory. Cullmann defends on historical and critical grounds the view that the "principalities and powers" of which Paul speaks are not only actual states and governments. They are the "supernatural powers" which stand behind these earthly powers. They are heavenly powers, which often become demonic in their rebellion. But Christ has defeated these powers, the New Testament says in Colossians, I Peter, and many other places. He reigns victoriously over them, though, to be sure, conflict must go on until all Christ's enemies have been put down. Here then in the New Testament is a view which sets Christ's reign above all earthly and heavenly powers which may turn against their creator and Lord. This puts the Christian in a position to challenge all claims to authority by the test of the mind of Christ. Dr. Visser 't Hooft quotes the prayer of the Dutch church which faced this problem not only as a theological issue, but as a matter of life and death for the Church. The prayer asks "that government may be so directed that the King of kings may rule over both rulers and subjects."

Gustaf Aulén, bishop of the Swedish Lutheran Church, carries through a similar thesis in his *Church, Law and Society*. He keeps the distinction so important to the whole outlook of the Reformation that the Gospel is not a new law. No legalistic prescription for Christian action can be derived from the New Testament message. But Aulén shows it is false to conclude from this that love in the Gospel is something separated from the demand for justice. Justice in the Biblical view is not a rational system of principles. It is the ordered will of God. We cannot formulate it in rules; but there is one principle: care for the neighbor. That is what God's justice requires. In short, for the Christian the work of justice is one with the work of love. In this sense love is the fulfillment of the law, as Paul says. Aulén vigorously argues that the function of human law is not only to restrain evildoers. It has the creative function of laying foundations for human fellowship. Dr. Conrad Bergendoff, American Lutheran theologian, in his *Christ as Authority* makes plain that out of the new relationship of the sinner justified by faith there must flow constructive Christian action in society. To know ourselves as men who depend wholly on the forgiveness of God means that we are bound to share the love we have received through the deeds in which we deal with our brothers.

While Lutheran ethics shows these trends away from a very sharp distinction of the realm of civil society from the realm of Christ's immediate reign and moral command, liberal Protestant ethics may be said to have moved from its extreme denial of this separation to a modified position. This movement has taken place through internal criticism from within the liberal position under the impact of the violence and social revolution of the first half of the twentieth century.

Liberal theology is the movement in modern Protestantism which tried to bring the Christian faith into unity with the spirit of idealistic culture, and the ideals of freedom and justice in the modern democratic movement. In Germany through the Ritschlian movement which had wide influence, and in the United States in the social gospel, liberals interpreted the Christian faith as leading to a program for the direct reformation of society and the establishment of Christian love as the foundation of a new social order. Sometimes the belief in "democracy" and the Christian faith were fused into one universal faith which identified the restoration of society according to the democratic pattern with the realization of the Kingdom of God. Sometimes the political order, with its democratic structure, was seen as the objective form of human community in which love for the neighbor would have the greatest freedom and creativity.

Liberalism produced a searching critique of modern industrial society. All the ways in which economic exploitation, racial prejudice, and anarchic international relations thwart and destroy the growth of persons were brought before the judgment of the Christian conscience by such men as the Anglicans F. D. Maurice and Charles Gore, and in America by Washington Gladden and Walter Rauschenbusch.

That liberalism fell into an unrealistic utopianism in these hopes for the good society is now generally agreed, though it should be remembered that as they worked within the perspective of an evolutionary view, liberals sometimes insisted on a very long time span for realization of the good world. The criticism of liberal optimism arose within liberalism itself. Reinhold Niebuhr's thought, beginning with his *Moral Man and Immoral Society* in 1932, has been of crucial effect in the reassessment of the liberal doctrines. His critique has caused a drastic reorientation of thinking on the relation of ethics to social policy and on the place of religious idealism both as a source of power and as a source of confusion.

Influenced by Reinhold Niebuhr, there is an able group of Christian interpreters of politics today engaged in showing how the evangelical understanding of man's sin and need of grace is relevant to politics precisely because it provides a doctrine of man which does not obscure the realities of social conflict. It rejects the sentimentality of trying to develop a political ethic which depends on the direct application of moral principle to every situation. It is "moralism," they argue, in the sense of an abstract ethic untouched by acquaintance with the power struggle in human groups which has confused and weakened Christian effectiveness in guiding social policy. Ernest Lefevre's book, *Ethics and United States Foreign Policy*, and John Bennett's *Christian Ethics and Social Policy*, are examples of this critique. They do not disavow the liberal affirmation that a social ethic can be derived from the Gospel; but they keep moral judgment within the perspective of man's involvement in the tragic ambiguities of history created by his finitude and by the self-centeredness which corrupts his life. The liberal impulse within this reassessment of the ethical problem should not be forgotten. Reinhold Niebuhr's analysis of democracy in *The Children of Light and the Children of Darkness*, and his appraisal of the vitalities and dilemmas of the American spirit in *The Irony of American History*, show how the social gospel gave an authentic element to the Christian witness even though it must be radically corrected by a realistic doctrine of man.

We have spoken of the Calvinist-Puritan tradition as the third ethical tradition in Protestantism. This is really a stream of many sources. It goes back to those groups in the Protestant Reformation on the Continent and in Britain who tried to work out the theocratic idea of the "human community under God." Some were Calvinists who formulated the role of the church in society to insure a genuinely free selection of rulers and ministers and yet preserve a central authority and order in the state. Those in the radical sects lived in excited anticipation of the new age in which ancient evils would be destroyed and a new order of life in freedom of the spirit would begin. From such sects as Diggers and Levellers, from Genevan Calvinists, from pioneer defenders of freedom for the mind such as John Milton, from Puritans and Pilgrims with their new ventures in America, from radical independents like Roger Williams, from the spiritual communities of the Friends, and from Deistic rationalists, the stream of the new impulse toward a union of spiritual freedom and responsibility broadened and flowed into the idealism of the modern democratic state.

It cannot be said that this stream had any obvious or simple unity. But what needs to be especially recognized is that in contrast to extreme Lutheranism and extreme liberalism the Calvinist spirit held together two important Christian ideas. On the one hand men are sinners, and all their relationships show the effects of sin. On the other hand men can be regenerated and human society can become an ordered commonwealth under the reign of God. The supremely important insight is that we can only deal intelligently with human problems when we take seriously both these truths. If we try to revise the laws and institutions of society without recognizing man's infinite capacity for self-seeking then we are naïve and we do not see what needs to be done. But if we remain passive before the monstrous evils of society then we have lost our faith in the God who reigns over all things, and who wills that society be transformed. For example, freedom is an ultimate value. Society should create institutions which give maximal freedom. But restraints on freedom are absolutely necessary, else the strong and ruthless will destroy the weak. History guarantees no inevitable progress. But specific evils like slavery can be attacked and destroyed. And in all things it must be remembered that a just society rests on the conscience and the mature wisdom of its members. Personal responsibility is a fundamental Protestant concept in politics and in the church.

Neither Calvinists nor sectarians escaped difficulties in living with these principles. New England Congregationalists established autocratic political communities. The Quakers' Holy Commonwealth became an ingrown and legalistic society, with tight control but dwindling spontaneity.[9] But this stream of thought remains a major resource for us today.

No traditional social philosophy is sufficient to cope with the gigantic new problems and powers which now dominate the human scene. But out of these Christian traditions a persistent Christian conscience is forging an ethical outlook which will bring a more adequate vision to guide the making of social policy. It will draw upon elements in all the views we have characterized. Its central theme is this: the God we know in Christ wills a just and brotherly community among all men. All human orders are subject to the judgment and the transforming power of love. But our life is determined not only by God's gracious love, but also by man's sinful pride, anger and greed. He who deals constructively with human problems must humbly accept the task of serving God in the midst of human frailty. Just because human institutions reflect human ignorance and evil those institutions will serve men best which involve the restraints and the procedures which are approriate to men as they are. How then does the Christian faith guide us in making practical judgments on human institutions? We must turn to see the lively debate now going on in Protestant theology over that question.

IV

We know the love of God in Jesus Christ. In his teaching and example we have the basic principle of "love for the neighbor." But the area of social relations involves settlements between conflicting groups, adjustments of human rights, work in political organization and action, endless bargaining, and even warfare. We seem to require a set of "middle principles" even to begin on these problems. How then do we move from the love of Christ to its fruits in specific ethical decisions? It is important to see that we can turn the question around. How does the struggle of the Christian conscience with problems of human society throw light on the meaning of the love which God has given in Christ? We can learn the meaning of Christian love only through living under its demand.

There are three reasons why we cannot solve the problem of Christian ethics by simply saying that love means finding out what our neighbor needs and doing it. The first is that it is not plain that "love" in the New Testament understanding is really an ethical principle or rule at all. It is a spirit. The *agape* of God is his own infinite care and mercy, giving itself utterly to draw men back to himself. If human love is an analogy for the divine, here also it is a spirit rather than a rule. Should Christian love be brought into the sphere of calculated duties and human claims according to rights? We must not lose the spirit by making it another law.

The second problem about Christian love has to do with the meaning of sacrifice. The revelation of God's love came to its climax when Jesus, having assumed the form of the servant, gave up his life on the cross. His self-giving was his service. But was it in any sense a self-realization? Jesus appears to serve no special political interest. He does not organize a military or political power to oppose other powers. He is crucified under the Roman Governor; but he enters into no political negotiation or controversy about rights or justice. On the cross he seems to bear the weight of the world's need in a love which the spirit of man cannot reckon. If God's love is here we can be saved by it; but how can we be guided by it in the human struggle for self-realization? What does it mean, for example, to speak of such self-giving in relation to the interests of a nation or even of a political party? There seems to be an incommensurability here. So the problem of self-sacrifice remains a central one for theology.

The third problem comes from the fact that we have to act in a world where evil has entered. Therefore we have the question of means and ends which may be necessary, but which involve contradictions of what love ultimately would seek. Our possessions and privileges divide us from our brothers. We resist in law court or in more deadly ways. And it seems to be the case that without this resistance life could not go on at all.

The problem of justice as it is related to love can best be stated here. No Christian moralist will argue that there is no place for justice in the Christian ethic. God is both just and merciful. God's "righteousness" in both Old Testament and New is practically synonymous with his loving care for all things. In God, justice and love are ultimately one. Therefore in principle the command to love is also a command to seek justice. But in the world as it is justice has to be worked out with the means and the compromises provided by conflicting social powers. If justice may be taken to mean, as H. N. Wieman holds, free and equal access to the sources of human fulfillment, then we know we get only a rough approximation of it.[10] What we do get comes largely through the give and take of human bargaining and battling. As Reinhold Niebuhr has frequently pointed out, we may deplore the fact that less than ideal means lead us to less than ideal ends. But most moral choices involve us in the use of far from perfect means.

The tension created in the moral life by acceptance of the claims of absolute love and the discovery of the contradiction which all life seems to offer to that spirit had led to some radical solutions in Christian history. Roman Catholicism has frankly accepted the view that the attempt to live by the absolute rule of love must be reserved to those who retire from ordinary life and its obligations, and adopt the religious vocation of monastic life. Lutheranism, as we have seen, has recognized a sharp distinction between the spirit of love and the realm of law. Liberal ethics saw that society as it is contradicts love, and asserted that the whole structure of life had to be changed to make love realizable. Anders Nygren sees the forgiving love of God, the *agape* of the New Testament, in sharp contrast to human *eros,* the worldly reason, passion, and idealism which tries to mount up toward fulfillment in the divine, but never escapes its own self-centeredness. *Agape* comes down freely and spontaneously from God. *Eros* tries to be fulfilled in an absolute good which includes the self.[11] Reinhold Niebuhr sharply distinguishes the sacrificial love revealed in Christ from the mutual love which seeks to include advantage to the self within the good of the other. He rejects the absoluteness of Nygren's distinction, however, and has devoted much of his work to an elaboration of the way in which a Christian ethic must make a place for justice as well as for love. Proximate norms, related to what is possible in human society, are absolutely essential for dealing with the relativities of human life. Classes and nations do not voluntarily surrender their privileges. But the knowledge of sacrificial love acts as a humbling and cleansing judgment.[12]

Emil Brunner accepts a sharp distinction also between love and justice.[13] He holds that love in the Christian sense is possible only in a fully personal relationship. Justice is concerned with rational and impersonal standards. Brunner rejects the attempt made in some postwar continental theology to derive law solely from the revelation in Christ.

For all these views theological ethics must show how love revealed in Christ is the final criterion and yet how the Christian ethic can incorporate the requirements of justice and order without which no human life is possible. How is this to be done?

V

There is a fairly sharp opposition between two different approaches to the doctrine of love in Christian ethics today. Each has its characteristic way of viewing the relation of love, law, and decision. After drawing this contrast we need to see how, under the influence of existentialist thought, a new perspective which may offer some transformation of both views is being introduced.

The first view makes a sharp distinction between the love revealed in Jesus Christ and all human love. It stresses the abyss between sacrificial love and all self-centeredness of spirit. As representative of this position I summarize briefly the argument of Paul Ramsey's very able *Basic Christian Ethics*. Ramsey stresses in a radical way the reversal which Christian love introduces into the ethics of self-realization. At the same time he is acutely aware of the resulting problems when the Christian sets out "in search of a social policy."

The clue to Ramsey's doctrine can be seen in his discussion of the commandment to "love thy neighbor as thyself." This saying has often been used to support the view that Christian ethics involves a proper "self-realization." Ramsey regards such an interpretation as a watering down of the radical character of the love taught by Jesus. What it means is that God's love requires an absolute self-giving to the good of the other. It does not calculate the consequences for the self. It reminds us of our usual attention to our own good, of the way in which we make our selves and our desires the center of all calculation, and it says that that is the kind of attention and concern you ought to give to your neighbor. Ramsey says, "The commandment requires the Christian to aim at his neighbor's good just as unswervingly as man by nature wishes his own. Thus Christian ethics draws its standard *from man* only by inverting it." Ramsey believes that "no more disastrous mistake can be made than to admit self-love onto the ground floor of Christian ethics as a basic part of Christian obligation, however much concern for self-improvement, for example, may later come to be a secondary, though entirely essential, aspect of Christian vocation."[14]

The "ground floor" of Christian ethics is a love which is completely self-giving. This doctrine is based, according to Ramsey, on the Bible's view of what God's love is. His discussion on this point is especially valuable because he emphasizes that the Biblical ideas of God's justice, his righteousness and his mercy are all interdependent. Certainly the Bible makes no final distinction between God's righteousness and his love. What is this righteousness? It is giving to men what they need. Ramsey interprets the Biblical notion of justice in the principle: "To each according to the measure of his real need, not because of anything human reason can discern inherent in the needy; but because his need alone is the measure of God's righteousness toward him."[15] So the Gospel brings a higher standard of judgment against all human calculation of values or preferential treatment according to the worth of men judged by human standards. Ramsey argues that this transcendent dimension of the Christian ethic sets it free to be an unconditional ethic for all historical situations. He further holds that it is love thus understood which alone can create human community where there is none. The ultimate problem of mankind is to find a basis for a genuinely human relationship in spite of the hates and fears, the isolation and the remembered injuries which destroy mutual relations. Obedient love can take the broken situation and bring healing and restoration. Self-love and mutual love may help to preserve community; but they cannot create it.[16]

Once this view of love is adopted we face serious questions about human rights and self-defense. And there is usually more than one neighbor. In order now to take another step toward a Christian social policy Ramsey says we need a definition of the nature of man. We have to have some basis for recognizing what human needs are. That means we must appropriate for Christian use some interpretation of the nature of man which comes from our own human self-understanding, that is, from philosophy. Ramsey is partial toward idealism as an aid to Christian ethics though he admits that idealism may be at some points inferior to a naturalistic philosophy in relation to the Biblical insights. In particular idealism tends toward a dualism between mind and body, with a corresponding tendency to exalt the higher faculties without regard to the corruption of sin at high spiritual levels. Still, idealism perceives at least these truths about man, that he has a conscience, that he has higher faculties with their creative possibilities, and that human reason possesses some understanding of the universal character of moral obligation. Kant's definitions of the moral law remind us that there is something in the structure of reason itself which leads us to see that every man must be treated as an end and not as a means alone.

One further step and we are ready to come to conclusions about problems of political ethics. We know that men are sinners. They violate their neighbors' good and have all manner of idealistic rationalizations of their powers and privileges. Therefore a Christian derivation of the structure of human rights will always be conscious both of the importance of setting men free to express their capacities and of providing effective restraints on irresponsibility.

Ramsey uses the problem of human rights to illustrate how Christian faith looks at social problems. Human rights do not inhere in the individual alone, they belong to him as one who can contribute to the group. "Marian Anderson has a right to sing in the Metropolitan Opera, not for Marian Anderson's sake as a private self, but for the sake of a better opera association, and for the sake of Marian Anderson as a contributor to the operatic art."[17] Many democratic rights are justified because they provide the necessary restraint on power. So Ramsey justifies universal suffrage. Counting all the votes is likely in the long run to insure that all interests will be heard. It is a way of bringing adequate pressure on those who would otherwise find good reasons to justify discriminatory treatment against some group. Ramsey quotes with approval Niebuhr's succinct statement, "Man's capacity for justice makes democracy possible; but man's inclination to injustice makes democracy necessary."[18]

Specific systems of rights may have many sources in human experience. But only through Christian love do we know what use to make of rights so that the community is served. Above all, Ramsey insists that Christian love must be kept free from identification with any law. Christian ethics may make coalitions with rational systems defining human values, but it must make "*concordats*" with no philosophy.[19] In the background of his assertion of the radical independence of the gospel of love lies a realistic discernment of the way in which even the highest thought can become the instrument of man's idolatrous overevaluation of his own interests.

VI

From St. Augustine to the present, there has been a tradition which seeks to bring all of man's ethical life, his self-love, his concern for justice, and the love which he receives from God into a more unified structure. This search for the unifying principle of moral experience in a love which embraces all of man's being leads to a particular dispute with the first view over the meaning of sacrifice in relation to self-love. In this Augustinian position the intent of all love, whether it be that of man for God, or God for man, or man for the neighbor, is the creation of a community in which all participate. To will the good of the other is not to deny the good of the self. It is to seek a new relationship in which each discovers his own good through intending the relationship of love with the other. Beginning with this basic position, this view has its characteristic way of approaching the problem of how Christian ethics can provide a place for self-regard, self-defense, and all the other practical requirements for a tolerable and just human community. Protestant interpreters of this position include John Macmurray, Henry N. Wieman, Gregory Vlastos, and others influenced by Whiteheadian philosophy.[20]

The issue drawn between the two doctrines may be illustrated by reference to the problem of self-defense, which Ramsey discusses. His justification for self-defense within the perspective of his doctrine of love is that one should defend himself for the sake of the neighbor. Thus even self-defense can be relieved of the taint of self-interest. Augustinians will be inclined to ask here, "Why is my life of worth to the neighbor?" Is it only because he is a neighbor that is someone other than myself, or is it because as a person he has worth and his needs ought to be met? But if my neighbor's life has a claim upon my concern, so has every life, including my own. Granted our unworthiness ever to have all that love gives to us, each self has at least this good: it is a potential member of the great community of beings related in love. Ramsey, of course, does not mean to deny the worth of human life. He says the Christian will find it salutary "to reflect a great deal upon man's great native potentialities."[21] The Augustinian doctrine would emphasize a positive evaluation of these potentialities and their importance in the basis of Christian ethics.

The problem of the Augustinian view is to show that it can avoid becoming a justification for personal selfishness. It is well known that men are bad judges in their own cases, just because each estimates his worth from a highly partial point of view. Does not Christian love turn our attention wholly away from our worthiness to receive it, and become a spontaneous giving of self without claims?

The issue is a profound one, but it may be observed that critics of the second position may overlook what it maintains. The important point is that this second view stresses the social character of human existence. There is no such thing as a good which belongs to one individual apart from his actual and potential relationships to others. Therefore, say the upholders of "community," Christian love can never be a matter of seeking my own good as something to be weighed over against the good of some other. I have no private good of my own. My good is only there in the sharing of the community in which I both give and receive. The one sure way for me to lose my own worth is to think I can have some exclusive and private good apart from my relationships to others. The conclusion can be stated as a principle: to seek a community of good which will be real for me means I must find that kind of relationship between self and community in which my own good comes through sharing my life with the whole.

We can begin now to see how this view deals with its central problem, the meaning of self-sacrifice. It holds that Christian love is sacrificial through and through. The question is, "What is it that is sacrificed?" Is it my whole self, or is it whatever there is in my self as it is which blocks my fuller participation in the community? If the latter then we can understand sacrifice without the negation of the self. And that is what this view holds. Christian love means the sacrifice of everything which comes between the self and its complete sharing of its life with the community of all selves. What the self is now, with all its petty or great ambitions, its little foothold of security in earthly goods, its own self-centered concern which does not regard the community first, all of this has to be surrendered. And this means that this earthly life itself may be given, and in the end must be given up for the larger community in which it shares. If my "self" is bound only to my own separate individuality as I live in this body in space and time, then giving up my life would indeed be a negation of the self. But the "self" is a participant in the ongoing community of life. I am what I belong to and what I serve. That does not die when this temporal and temporary self dies.

Actually no Christian ethic demands that every Christian give up his life completely here and now. Why not? Because it would destroy this precious community of human existence. But every Christian ethic holds that every Christian may at some time serve God best by giving up his life. Why? Because in this world as it is the growing community of good must sometimes be served by those who die that it may go on. We all die. The ethical question is the manner in which our death as well as our life may serve God's purpose.

This "community" theory of love as worked out in Protestant theology today comes to a very similar judgment on specific questions of political order and human rights as does the "sacrificial" view. The "community" theory perhaps leads more directly to a Christian social philosophy. Wherever any values of human life in community are involved, there the Christian spirit sees a positive good to be developed and served. But every human community is to be judged from the standpoint of how the actual relationships within it either serve or block the growing freedom of each member and his capacity to share in the whole community of persons. All the basic democratic freedoms of religion, of speech, of political participation can be derived from this one all-inclusive freedom and right of the human spirit under God to enter fully into the possibilities of a life in which the good of each is bound up forever with the good of all.

For this second position as for the first, any legalistic definition of human rights, or any fixed prescription of human obligations and ethical codes is rejected. It is the concrete good in human relations that counts. That is full of uncertainties, mysteries, and dynamic personal factors which no law can possibly anticipate. The community which love seeks is not a fixed ideal pattern. It is an ever-unfolding and infinitely rich reality. To serve that and that alone is to know the freedom of the Gospel from the law and yet to remain responsible toward all law which helps to guide life into such a community.

There is no intention in this second position of denying the tragic character of our actual moral choices, and of our situation clouded as it is by our own sin. Life presents us with choices in which goods and evils are so mixed that even without the darkness of our own self-will we would have to confess our involvement in great evil, and our continuing dependence on God's redemptive grace which saves the goodness of life in spite of its evil.

VII

Since the end of the second world war the world has undergone sweeping changes brought about by revolutionary forces, both technological and political. Human problems have taken on new and awesome proportions, partly under the threat of nuclear war, partly because of the sharp edge put upon human hopes through the new powers given by scientific knowledge. Population explosion, revolutionary nationalism, the confrontation of communism in its Russian and Chinese embodiments with the liberal democracies of the west have all produced unprecedented issues in the strategies of national survival, and the search for a workable human community. Every society is undergoing profound stresses. In the affluent society of the United States the unsolved problems of civil rights and poverty have produced new forms of political movements, and the manifestation of non-violent strategies and violent reprisals.

The Christian church has not escaped the growing sense that the ethical traditions of the past, whatever honor we give to them, may not be sufficient to cope with the new demands on the human conscience. The principles of natural law, of philosophical idealism, of pragmatic utilitarianism all betray weakness in answering the question: how shall man survive and achieve the new order of life which science has now made possible? Let us look at some critical points where the search for a new ethical perspective is required.

First, there is the collapse of the ideal of "Christendom." Traditional Christian ethics has tended to assume that the goal of the Church is the construction of an ordered society according to Christian principles, or at least of a society which would express in an indirect way the ideals of the Christian view of life. But today Christian moralists of many different communions would say that the idea of Christendom is now not so much wrong as irrelevant. The church exists in civilizations everywhere in the world which are shaped by technical and political forces which cannot by any stretch of imagination be said to reflect or accommodate particular religious traditions. Old stabilities are swept away. New forms of human society, new kinds of adjustment and social control are manifest everywhere which make no obeisance to past ethical or religious forms. What shape the new societies will take no one knows. The problem seems to be not to impose a plan derived from a traditional outlook but to see what is viable, hopeful, and responsible, given the new forces released in society by technical productivity, the population explosion, weapons of destruction, and the passionate mass movements toward new national dignity. In this new world the church has a distinctive witness, but not in the form of a pattern for a Christian order.

A second challenge follows immediately upon the first. A new secularism is offering a way of life which embodies human values, and which makes no claims for religious support. The secular outlook, with its pursuit of concrete values, its confidence in human intelligence, and its resistance to ecclesiastical authority is of course nothing new. A secularist humanism with a positive basis for human action toward rational goals has been a continuous option in western civilization, and in the eastern tradition also. We recall that the dominant mood of the theological movement between the two World Wars was highly critical of this secular optimism. It pointed to the biblical view of the judgment of God upon all human schemes, and the necessity of man's acceptance of his dependence upon grace as the ground of all truly humane ethics. It is characteristic of the theological mood in the latter part of the century that there is a reversal of this attitude toward the secular standpoint. The new theological ethics is more afraid of irrelevance than it is of over-optimism. It sees Christianity as bringing insight, judgment, and renewal to man's life, but this can be done only as the church and the Christian take responsibility within the secular world, discovering how secular man meets his problems, and joining in the struggle for some human way of dealing with them. An influential statement of the new mood is given by Harvey Cox, a Christian sociologist, in *The Secular City:*

In the age of the secular city, the questions with which we concern ourselves tend to be mostly functional and operational. We wonder how power can be controlled and used responsibly. We ask how a reasonable international order can be fashioned out of the technological community into which we have been hurried. . . . These are pragmatic questions and we are pragmatic men whose interest in religion is at best peripheral.

As for answers to these questions Cox says:

Secular man relies on himself and his colleagues for answers. He does not ask the church, the priest, or God. . . .[21]

Secular man has always relied upon himself, but what is noteworthy in the new Christian ethic is that the source of ethical insight for the Christian is believed to be bound up with understanding this secular standpoint, and while not wholly adopting it finding how the Christian faith can bring significant guidance in the secular tasks. Cox finds support in Professor Amos Wilder's remark that any sense of transcendence today will have to be experienced in and through the secular. Cox believes that God is encountered in the boundary situations of social action. He says it might be well to call a moratorium on the use of the word God for a time, but it is possible that God and man may "find joy together in doing a common task." [22] This phrase sounds remarkably like a restoration of the once scorned liberal doctrine that man may cooperate with God in the task of world-making.

If Christian ethics is to find its foundation in the assertion that man cooperates with God, then Christian decisions must follow from some discernment of what God is doing in the world. How does the Christian get his criterion for what he is to do?

An answer to this question is being given in Christian theology which is variously called "situational ethics" or "contextual ethics." It derives from the reexamination of the ethical problem in the light of the biblical faith and the search for a new freedom of response to the demands of meeting the neighbor in love in the concrete new situations. The new ethical position is a radical restatement of the traditional search for the right relation of law and Gospel, and the problem is resolved in a radical freedom to respond in love to need without benefit of the formulation of general principles of action. It is the concrete human situation which has to be met and this cannot be grasped in abstract principles.

Dr. H. Richard Niebuhr's ethics which he expounded in teaching, but which is only partially available in his published writings, stressed the personal context of moral obligation. He believed that the Christian answer to the problems of defining the goal of ethical behavior and the forms of moral obligation must be derived within the life of the responsible self whose real context is the relationship between God and man. The responsible self discovers specific obligation by responding to the good which emerges in personal community through loyalty, love, and critical judgment. Thus Richard Niebuhr's ethics always made a point of contact with the usual philosophic definition of the forms of ethics as the search for the good, and of the principles of duty. But he held that Christianity has the fully personal and adequate answer as to how and where the good is to be found. It is therefore an ethic of value, but the values are derived from the personal context.[23]

Such a contextualist position has been given a new thoroughgoing statement in Professor Paul Lehmann's *Ethics in a Christian Context*. He develops the position of Richard Niebuhr, of Karl Barth and of Dietrich Bonhoeffer in a systematic analysis of the distinctive character of a Christian ethic whose context is the Christian community brought into being through God's act in Jesus Christ. Christian responsibility takes its direction solely from the Christian understanding of how God acts through Jesus Christ for the redemption of the world. The term "Koinonia ethics" (community ethics) is sometimes used to characterize this position when we understand that community means the Christian community understood from the perspective of the evangelical faith. A brief summary of the cardinal points in Lehmann's thesis will be useful.

The theological perspective of Lehmann's contextualist doctrine is informed by the Calvinist theme of the sovereignty of God and his will to judge, order and redeem the world. God's way with man is that of the redemptive love which creates in Jesus Christ a new community of life out of the wreckage brought about by sin. While we cannot read the divine will directly out of our perception of events, we know through Christ that its goal is the fulfillment of humanity in the new community which God intends. Dr. Lehmann therefore speaks of the "politics of God" as the guiding image for ethical interpretation. He uses "politics" here of course in the classical and root sense of "statecraft." The Christian knows that the "state to be created" is God's kingdom. This cannot be defined by criteria drawn from any other political outlook than that of Christian faith itself.

The Christian community can claim no absolute knowledge of the "politics of God" or what this implies in specific political decisions; but it is the Christian community which is the nurturing context for the conscience. Christian action therefore is the expression of the will to reconciliation with the neighbor. It is personal concern in action. "It is through the life of the Christian community that we are enabled to see the neighbor as he is," Professor Lehmann says. "It is from and within the Christian koinonia that conscience acquires ethical reality and the power to shape behavior through obedient freedom." [24] No absolute claims should be made for the empirical church, but it is the locus in the world of the formative reality which leads to the ethical relationship to the neighbor:

the empirical church points, despite its ambiguity, to the fact that there is in the world a laboratory of the living word, or to change the metaphor, a bridgehead of maturity, namely the Christian *Koinonia* (community).[25]

The situationalist or contextualist position here developed is not a purely individualistic one. It is through life in the community informed by grace that the personal conscience is tempered and directed. But what is the conscience directed toward? This is the critical question.

The content of moral action is defined by Professor Lehmann through use of the concept of "humanization." God is making human life human, and we are to be obedient to that action. "All things are instrumental to the doing of the will of God as God himself guides and shapes the conscience through the dynamics and direction of what he himself is doing in the world to make human life human." [26]

In this position then the Christian is free to seek in every concrete situation what is required that the growth toward maturity of human beings may be furthered. Lehmann here refers to Dietrich Bonhoeffer in an illustration of what is involved in telling the truth. In a brief work entitled "What does it Mean to Tell the Truth," Bonhoeffer says that telling the truth

> is a matter of accurate and serious consideration of the actual circumstances. The more complex the circumstances of a man's life are, the more responsible he is; and the more difficult it is for him to tell the truth. Therefore, telling the truth must be learned . . . since it is simply a fact that the ethical cannot be detached from the real situation, the increasingly accurate knowledge of the situation is a necessary element of ethical action.[27]

The contextualist asks us to consider the problems involved for doctors dealing with disturbed patients, politicians running campaigns, soldiers in war, teachers encouraging students yet trying not to arouse false hopes, spies loyally serving their country, writers of advertising copy, parents helping children to discover the real world without being terrified by it. Do we not recognize how important the element of humanisation, of telling the truth in love really is? As Bonhoeffer says it is a matter of the "right word; the living word which is as alive as life itself."

We still need a criterion of the "human," else ethics is left to the intuition or whim of the moment. Here Professor Lehmann sees the answer for Christian faith in Christology, for Jesus is the new mature humanity incarnate. The messianic dimension in the understanding of the incarnation is stressed by Lehmann. Christ brings the humanity which "is to be." He points forward in the creative history where God is at work toward the new humanity God is creating and which is found in the organic relationship of Christ the Head and the members of his body.

This contextualist position opens the way to a fresh examination of every issue of human responsibility in a way which transcends the application of traditional rules or principles. It asserts the force of a sense of responsibility which transcends formal obligation in favor of concrete need. It leaves certain issues which are at present being vigorously debated. We mention three.

First, an ethic without principles sounds free and flexible, but can it answer the question "what ought we to do?" Certainly we should act justly, out of love. But what is doing justly? If there is no answer to that question in terms of principle then any question concerning rights, equality, mutuality would seem to be settled by asking the question, how can I now act to secure justice. But whose justice? If I answer only in terms of the "new humanity" do I not have to describe this humanity in ways which look very much like ethical principles? For example, I do not have to recreate the standard of the freedom, dignity and claim to equal treatment of each person in every ethical act. Are there not rules which do apply, however complex their application?

An American philosopher, William K. Frankena, has given a useful distinction between rule-agapism and act-agapism in his analysis of Christian ethics.[28] The question is, can a pure act-agapism escape the need for some rational articulation of the terms upon which we are required to act. Paul Ramsey has raised this question in an extensive critique of Lehmann's contextualist ethics.[29] Ramsey argues that Lehmann's interpretation of the dropping of the atomic bomb on Hiroshima and Nagasaki as an exceptional act, which shows how the Christian conscience must transcend all prescription, really reduces justification of ethical action to secular interest and need.[30] Ramsey still wants to look for ultimate principles governing the ethical use of power, and has been exploring this in a variety of contexts including sexual ethics, the strategies of non-violence, and the ethical issues in the use of nuclear weapons.[31]

Roman Catholic moralists have vigorously entered the discussion of the situations ethics, and have shown considerable hospitality to the emphasis on the responsibility of conscience in dealing with the concrete situation. But they also argue that for the conscience to rely solely on love as it makes its response in the situation is to leave the matter of ethical judgment solely to inward feeling. Some objective norms for "loving" behavior formulated in ethical principles are necessary guides to the conscience, not only in judging others, but in judging onself. A sharp statement of the issues involved here is found in a discussion of the new morality between the protestant Joseph Fletcher and the Roman Catholic Herbert McCabe.[32] Fletcher holds that "nothing is inherently good or evil, except love (personal concern and its opposite, indifference or actual malice)." McCabe argues for the necessity of objective principles which express the commitments and sensitivities of love, such as faithfulness to the person, respect for human dignity and equality. He acknowledges that the Church is in desperate need of a new moral theology and there is as yet hardly any sign of it. The out-

standing Catholic theologian Karl Rahner has called attention to
the danger of a complete interiorization of the standard of ethics.
Man after all remains sinner in spite of love and grace. He needs
the guidance of principles.

A second defense of ethical principles not wholly bound to situations is based upon the nature of personal commitments and the
foundations of fidelity and trust in social life. How can the faithfulness in the marriage vow, the pledge of life, fortune and sacred
honor in the foundation of the national community, the honoring
of the relationships between parents and children, teachers and
students, doctors and patients, elected officials and citizens be established unless there are principles which are respected as part of the
fabric of human relationships? William Ernest Hocking has pointed
out that what men seek in relation to one another is in one aspect
precisely the discovery of the terms upon which they can live with
one another. Situational ethics may be deficient because in relegating
principles to the periphery it has failed to recognize the extent to
which man is a principle-seeking being.

A third question is closely related to the other two. It arises from
the practical circumstance that the human communities today are
either dominated by such secular political forces as communism, or
they are pluralistic societies where the basis for law, for constitu-
tions, for the common life cannot be established by appeal to one
religious tradition. The context is that of many religious communities or none at all. How does the Christian find a basis for political judgment and cooperation with those whose presuppositions
are quite different? The dilemma of the situation ethic at present
is that it appeals to the Christian community at a time when the
ideal of Christendom is irrelevant. The actual context of behavior
is the secular community. How this gap is to be bridged in a Christian situations ethic has not yet been made clear.

These issues are pressing in the realm of human law where an increasingly vigorous theological and ethical discussion is now taking place.

VIII

We have seen that Roman Catholic moralists have been reexamining the concept of natural law. Protestant theories of law have on the whole been critical of natural law doctrines, especially as presented in Catholic thought, but it cannot be said that Protestant theory has produced a compelling alternative. Hence the subject of the theological basis of law has entered a new and vigorous discussion in which conversation between Catholics and Protestants plays an increasingly large role.

In the past, Protestant theories of law have been of two main types. In one the state is seen as having its special structure and norms determined ultimately by God, but not subject to the direct application of the principles of Christian love. The state belongs to the orders of creation which are ordained by God to make life possible and tolerable, especially in view of sin, but the conditions and forms of these orders do not directly yield to the new life implied by the Kingdom of God. A second view is the idealistic one that Christianity has a vision of society ruled by justice and informed by love. Here the law of the state is seen as a primary instrument for ordering the common life so that something akin to the Christian society will be achieved.

Neither of these views finds much support at the present time, at least in their extreme forms. Protestant thought has faced, as Catholic thought has also had to, the problems of social policy and compromise, of the relativity of moral judgment, the concompatibility of various systems of law with the spirit of justice and love. At the same time there is recognition that Christian responsibility involves facing the problems encountered in the administration of law, and using the forms of legal institutions and the content of law as a field in which human values are to be sought and supported. The orders are not fixed.

The lively debate about the nature of law has produced two main lines of thought. They may be characterized by using two of the types of relationship of Christ to culture which Richard Niebuhr designated. The first sees Christ and culture in paradoxical tension, and the second sees Christ as the converter of culture.[33]

The first position sees the Gospel and the law as two realities, separated by the gulf created by human sin. One of its ablest exponents is Jacques Ellul, Protestant professor in the University of Bordeaux. He would eliminate all metaphysical and idealistic concepts of law for law "is a collection of human laws, made by men and applied by men." [34] We should not make the Gospel into a law, even a higher law. Love is not a principle with which other principles are to be criticized. The Gospel is the reality of life in grace given in Jesus Christ to sinful men. Therefore the Christian attitude toward law should be one which Ellul calls "realism," that is understanding law as it actually operates without overtones of idealistic justification or superior sanction. "Realism leads us finally to admit that it is unthinkable to found a legal system on Christian love or to translate it into formulas of Law." [35] The Christian can work within the structures of society seeking to express there the liberality and spontaneity of the love of God by respecting and using law, but always under the judgment of the Christian understanding of man's real situation. The Christian can see, in the light of the Gospel, the true ground of law in the justification of man given by God in Jesus Christ. It is significant that Ellul, like the American William Stringfellow with whom he closely agrees, comes out strongly for a situations ethic. The Christian must exhibit imagination, inventiveness, and initiative, and avoid stereotypes. Thus the practical outcome of this sharp separation of Gospel and law seems to result in a pragmatic and utilitarian stance. In a recent paper

Ellul gives an astute analysis of the relation of law to the process of human valuation. Law finds its force in the fact that it *represents* what men value and it has its power as an instrument for securing what is valued. Here Ellul seems to offer a basis for a Christian view of law which makes some contact with a more general and secular jurisprudence.[36]

William Stringfellow keeps the tension between Gospel and law at very nearly its absolute point. He says that "the tension between law and grace is such that there is no Christian jurisprudence." There is no philosophy of law which has special approval in the Gospel. The law cannot save and it cannot establish justice. But the Christian is not indifferent to it. Mr. Stringfellow, himself a lawyer, has given his professional life to defending the dispossessed in a great city. It is, he says, a matter of vocation. The Christian can enter into the problems of men as they are affected by law and make his witness there. But the sole vocational decision is "to be a Christian." The real context of Christian life is the body of Christ, the Church in the world. Therefore there is the closest relationship between the Christian community and its liturgy, and the source of political wisdom and action.[37]

This position which sets law and Gospel at such extremes has roots in Karl Barth's theology for both Ellul and Stringfellow. Many Christian theologians and philosophers of law would prefer what in Richard Niebuhr's language we may call the conversionist position. This group would grant much of what is said about the extra-Christian, secular, and pragmatic basis of actual legal structure. They would acknowledge further that there can be no direct creation of a Christian form of law, or a Christian state, but they believe that the Gospel must make contact with the ethical sense of mankind, and with those aspects of legal justice which can be both supported and transformed in the light of the Christian understanding of justice. Wilbur Katz, Paul Ramsey, Samuel Stumpf would appear to share, with variations, such a viewpoint. It has remained for one who is not a theologian but a legal philosopher, Edmond Cahn, to give one of the most powerful statements of the resources within the development of the legal process itself for discovering and establishing human values which must be ultimately approved from the point of view of the biblical tradition. In his books, *The Sense of Injustice* and *The Moral Decision,* Professor Cahn argued that in the legal tradition there is an evolving insight into the issues which concern human justice, privacy, equality, and responsibility.[38] He does not place his confidence in legal institutions alone, but in the slow growth of humane insight which is nourished by the sense of injustice and which is articulated now both in law and in the moral tradition. Cahn never denies the relevance of religious faith to moral sensitivity. But he does point out that the legal process, when it has had a measure of freedom to express the human sense of injustice, has often arrived at a sensitivity on moral issues which religious institutions themselves have sometimes lacked. This point does not, it seems to the present writer, get adequate recognition from the school of Ellul and Stringfellow. It is a clear case where the relation of the Church to the world should lead the Church to a certain humility about claiming any monopoly on the knowledge of justice.

Many specific issues where law and morality meet are being faced in the new discussion of law both by Protestants and Catholics. Glanville Williams in *The Sanctity of Life and the Criminal Law* has surveyed the relations of theology, law and ethics in such issues as birth control, sterilization, and euthanasia, and has effectively documented the difficulty of arriving at precise rules to cover either historic practice or the sensitivities of the conscience in these areas.[39] A theological interpretation of the ethical questions involved in medical practice is given in Joseph Fletcher's *Morals and Medicine,* which stresses the values of personal freedom and responsibility as interpreted in a Christian perspective in dealing with the issues.[40] There is increasing interest in the meeting of lawyers and theologians in a discussion of the foundations of law and of the myriad concrete questions which are posed as men try to cope with the new problems and possibilities of a technological civilization. Clearly both legal theory and the theology of law are due for a far reaching re-examination.

We see that the Christian spirit can generate a variety of ethical outlooks. If we look for the unity and integrity of the Christian perspective on moral obligation we shall find it only in the spirit of love as this is expressed in responsibility for the neighbor and the freedom to exercise that responsibility under the conditions created both by man's bearing the image of God and his sin. Thus love leads to involvement in the ambiguous processes of human living and social action. God's work in the world often has the "strangeness," as Luther called it, which involves the mystery of evil and the tragedies of history.

The Christian ethic can take both conservative and revolutionary forms, and both at the same time. It can lead to the elaboration of principles of moral obligation, but can also declare radical freedom to cope with unprecedented situations. Every system of Christian ethics come finally under the judgment of God's creative and redemptive work which cannot be captured in any formal system. It is a work of reconciliation which looks to the creation of a new order which will not be perfect, but which may reflect with more adequacy those human relationships and obligations of man to man, and of man within nature which are appropriate for creatures of the God who wills a community of life for all.

Such hope in history involves a faith about the meaning of history. We come to the central question for Christian faith: How do we understand what has happened to the world in Jesus of Nazareth, who, Christians say, is the Christ?

CHAPTER V

Jesus Christ in History and Faith

CHRISTIAN thought about God and man is determined by the accounting we give of who Jesus Christ is and what he does. Donald Baillie has well said, "Christianity is not theism plus Christology."[1] We do not simply add some beliefs about Christ to other beliefs. He transforms our beliefs. The ages of the world and the life of the spirit are divided into the time before Christ and the "new age of our Lord." Paul says, "Have this mind in you which was also in Christ Jesus." So Christian theology prepares for Christology, or is Christology, or follows out the implications of Christology.

This accounting the Church gives of its Lord is never finished. Through Christ we have a new understanding of how revelation and mystery imply each other. But while the mystery of Christ remains, we try to say precisely what we do know of him. It has always been difficult, and modern knowledge has brought new perplexities. The historical and critical understanding of the Bible; the conception of the laws of nature which makes untenable for us some aspects of the ancient world view; new knowledge of human psychology and of the psychology of religious movements, are some of the factors which lead to rethinking of the Christological faith. Some theologians believe it requires a radical recasting of the form if not the spirit of much traditional dogma.

My aim in this chapter is to show how the questions about Jesus Christ are being formulated today, and then to examine certain radical attempts to bring our knowledge of Christ into intelligible unity with our knowledge of nature and history. I hope to show

how out of the very perplexity of theology today some new insight is being derived into the nature of the revelation of God in Christ.

I

We need to remind ourselves of what it is that the Christian faith has always asserted about Jesus Christ. God has given his truth and saving power to the world through one man in whom God is present in a unique and complete way. The "Saviour" in the Christian faith is God and man together. This idea marks Christian faith off from all others. Many religions have "saviours." Many ancient faiths have dying and rising gods. But in the New Testament He who dies and rises is truly man as well as God. His death is not a "straw death." Other religions have looked to the coming of a Christ. They have expected God to act in history to redeem it. The faith of the Old Testament finds its ultimate expression just in this hope. But as Reinhold Niebuhr says, the Christ who came is not the Christ who was expected.[2] He does not fulfill either the national or the religious hopes of any culture or religion in the way in which they expect the fulfillment. Jesus stands in the line of the Old Testament prophets, and his message is in large part theirs. But in Christian faith he not only speaks the word of God, he is the word of God. In the words of the Nicene Creed, he is the "enmanned God."

Whatever our attitude toward the ancient creeds, we recognize that throughout Christian history the words of the Chalcedonian formula have held the two sides of the Christian affirmation together. At Chalcedon (A.D. 451) the Council declared that our Lord Jesus Christ "is at once complete in Godhead and complete in manhood, truly God and truly man," and that he is "one and the same Christ, Son, Lord, Only-begotten recognized in two natures, without confusion, without change, without division, without separation . . . the characteristics of each nature being preserved and coming together to form one person and subsistence."

This doctrine of the two natures was the basis for the doctrine of his saving work. On the Cross this God-man dies and brings God's love to redemptive encounter with human need. It is noteworthy that the Church never achieved authoritative definition of the Atonement. There have been many theories of Christ's work. But there have also been many theories of his Person in spite of the definition of Chalcedon. There has been a continual restlessness in the Christian mind about what this unity of two natures in one person means.

It is fair to say that in the history of Christian thought as it has worked out from the Chalcedonian formula, with its background of a world picture with two realms, one natural and one supernatural, the greatest difficulty has been to assure that the real humanity of Jesus is affirmed. The Gospel record asserts that he grows in wisdom and stature. He becomes tired, hungry, thirsty. He is tempted, he prays, and wrestles in spiritual agony over his supreme decision. He dies. Among the traditional attempts to be faithful to these facts and yet to assert Jesus' divinity are theories of *krypsis,* the hiding of the divine attributes, and *kenosis,* the divesting of the incarnate Son of some of his divine powers. One strongly held tradition declares that it was "human nature" as an impersonal universal, and not a particular human nature which the Lord assumed.

We are talking obviously about interpretations of the incarnation. There is a growing insistence in theology today that if we are to bring any clarity into Christology we have to show how we distinguish and relate historical facts, interpretation of the facts, and the role of faith in creating and judging the interpretation. Dr. John Knox puts the matter succinctly by saying that our Gospel record shows how Jesus was "remembered, was known still, and was interpreted."[3] The Gospels give us a history, Jesus' words are recorded. His deeds are told. There was the man, "crucified under Pontius Pilate." The Gospels also interpret these happenings. They tell us something of Jesus' interpretation of his mission, and they give us the interpretation of the first Christian communities. It is by no means easy to separate Jesus' self-interpretation from that of the community. And it is very difficult to separate the "actual historical facts" from the meaning of those facts as seen in faith. An outstanding example is the account of the resurrection. What here is "fact" and what reflects the Christian community's faith about the meaning of the facts? Both Knox and C. C. Morrison stress that it is this interrelation of Jesus with the community of believers that really "carries" the revelation of God. In Knox's words: "It was in Jesus *as known in the church* both before his death and afterwards, that the fresh activity of God among men which we call the revelation in Christ first occurred."[4]

If Christian faith were simply an idea which happened to come into the world through certain historical events, we could quite easily dismiss the problem of history and interpretation. But it is a faith about God's action in history. This character of the Christian faith is clearly seen when we consider the outcome of the attempt made at one stage in the modern discussion to distinguish between "the Jesus of history" and the "Christ of faith." Some who pressed this distinction wanted to separate Jesus as ethical teacher and revelation of the "immanent" spirit of God from Paul's interpretation of the Son of God who redeems the world through his death on the Cross. To be sure, Paul's interpretation of Christ goes beyond anything recorded of Jesus' thought, and it goes beyond the Gospel writers. But Paul's faith depends absolutely upon the assertion that the Christ he is talking about has come in the history of Jesus of Nazareth.

In his recent *God Was in Christ* Donald Baillie has clearly stated what is at stake in keeping history and faith together. He says, "The phrase 'Jesus of history' means simply and precisely: 'Jesus as He really was in His life on earth,' which includes, of course, what He did, and said, what He intended, and what He taught." Baillie goes on to point out that " 'Jesus as He really was' must not be taken to mean 'Jesus as a figure which can be described and authenticated by a cold criticism' for that would not be real history at all."[5] It means Jesus in his full and active relationship to man and to God. We can say nothing about that without interpreting the facts and in the process declaring our faith.

Two observations about the present stage of the discussion of history and faith are pertinent. The first is that the result of the "quest of the historical Jesus" as told by Albert Schweitzer in his epoch-making book of that title has left us with a picture of Jesus of Nazareth which does not fit easily into the traditional supernatural dogma about his Person. Since Schweitzer showed that Jesus could not be understood apart from his own expectation of the imminent end of the world, we have had to reckon with a real discrepancy between some aspects of his world view and ours. Schweitzer's specific reconstruction of Jesus' thought has been qualified and modified by critics in many ways, especially his estimate of the significance of this eschatology for Jesus' ethical teaching. But his book still marks a turning point. Historical research both implies and leads to the picture of Jesus as a man who participates in the historically conditioned culture and ideas of his particular time and place. Those who begin here are likely to have a Christology which preserves the humanity of Jesus. But how then is God present in a unique way in him?

The second observation concerns a shift in the terms in which the Christological problem is now formulated. The creeds unite the divine and supernatural nature with the human and earthly existence. The conviction that such a union has taken place was bound to be supported in large part by reference to miracles and other supernatural signs. Christ shows who he is by the exercise of extraordinary powers. But for those who are now driven by the critical understanding of Christian origins to a new view of the problem, the terms have subtly shifted. It is not two "natures" which have to be related; but two "histories." There is the history of our human existence with its fate, its freedom, and its course of events. In this history stands the real person, Jesus of Nazareth, who is just as truly "historical" as any other. There is also the history of God's creative and redemptive dealing with men which has come to its climax in the history of Jesus. It is these two histories which we have to relate to each other. When we look for God's redemptive action it is not supernatural existence but personal meaning which concerns us. The emphasis on miracle gives way to that on personal faith. To use H. Richard Niebuhr's terms in *The Meaning of Revelation,* in Jesus Christ outer and objective history has come together with inner and personal history which is known by faith. It may well be that this shift in the terms of the Christological problem is more important for theology today than any of the particular solutions which have yet been put forth.

II

Let us follow this interpretation of Jesus Christ at the intersection of two histories to see how it is being worked out today, and to see what the characteristic problem of this type of Christology is. There can be no doubt that theologians have found in this distinction between objective factual knowledge and personal grasp of meaning a potent means of saving theology from the disintegrating effect of a narrow and positivistic historicism. They have appropriated the theme of existentialism that the actual nature of our existence is known only through the free decision and risk of the human spirit in confronting our insecure and temporal life. How this conception of the significance of Jesus becomes meaningful for faith can be clearly seen in the analysis of Mr. Allan Galloway's recent book, *The Cosmic Christ*. The very difficult problem of the effect of the redemption wrought in Jesus Christ upon the whole creation is taken up by Mr. Galloway. How can events on this earth at a certain date affect the whole order of sun and stars, and indeed the other spiritual beings who may inhabit other universes? The New Testament says that in Christ the whole cosmos is redeemed and all its powers are brought under subjection to him. We do have one instance of the relation of spirit to the impersonal order of nature. Our bodies function in the material order, yet express personal meanings there. But our bodies affect the cosmos very slightly if at all beyond our immediate environment. How then can we think of the effect of a happening in the human history of Jesus upon the impersonal powers and structures of the world which seem largely indifferent or hostile?

To solve the problem Galloway turns to the existential personalist analysis. He follows Tillich closely when he points out that "self and world" forms the basic correlation in human existence. The meaning of the world comes to us interlocked with our own self-understanding. Whatever we find in our self, we find it bound up in the whole world order. Therefore, in an existential way we can say that every happening in the personal order does change the "impersonal order of nature." That is to say, it alters the self-world correlation. There is sickness in the world. Animals and human beings are subject to it. But it is what sickness *means to us* which is the concrete reality for our personal existence and our faith. The coming of the Christ is an event in the self-world correlation. In this sense the redemption he brings is redemption of the whole cosmos. He has redeemed all the cosmos which has any meaning for us, that is the one which participates in the struc-

ture of our personal existence. Of course for Galloway our knowledge of this redemption depends wholly upon our personal
recognition of what the Christ means. We can believe it "only on
the immediate evidence of the personal religious encounter with
the Christ Himself—either as the Christ in the flesh or as the
resurrected Christ."[6]

We can see here how the Christian faith is held together with
our contemporary knowledge of history and nature. We are relieved
of the intolerable burden of anxiety concerning historical researches
into the details of Jesus' existence. As Dr. Tillich says, the Christian cannot live as if every morning the mail might bring news of
historical researches which discredit the Christian faith. Christ is
a reality in our personal encounter with those "facts" which gave
rise to the life of the Church. That faith no historical research
can shake. Again, this personal conception of faith relieves us of
the impossible task of trying to prove by reference to purely
objective data the reality of God. It is possible to look at the facts
of existence and see no meaning there which discloses any God.
Unless our spirits are brought to a sense of our dependence so that
we acknowledge the creative source of life, and unless our own
self-knowledge opens our minds to find meaning in the forgiveness
which is offered to us, the Christian faith will simply appear
meaningless. Historical events do not bestow their ultimate significance upon us apart from our own personal involvement. In
Chapter I we have seen how some historians are stressing this
point. For theology it is of utmost importance that only "eyes of
faith," in Paul Minear's phrase, can see truly who Jesus was.

Every Christological position has its difficulties. The moment we
lean too far in emphasizing the personal aspect of faith, we may
begin to discount the importance of the objective facts. Donald
Baillie has summarized the evidence that there is in the position
we are just now considering a tendency to depreciate the significance

for Christian faith of the actual series of events which took place in and around the life of Jesus. Søren Kierkegaard gives us a useful illustration of the danger because he put it in such an extreme way. He said: "If the contemporary generation had left behind them nothing but the words, 'we have believed that in such and such a year God appeared among us in the humble figure of a servant, that He lived and taught in our community and finally died,' it would be more than enough."[7] Probably no contemporary theologian would put this so extremely. But an echo of this position is certainly to be found in Barth's famous dictum that behind the New Testament picture of the Christ we can see only the "Rabbi of Nazareth," rather unexceptional alongside many other religious figures.[8]

In *The Mediator* Emil Brunner says that the Deity of Christ which is the secret of his Person "as such does not enter into the sphere of history at all."[9] Critics of this book found Brunner very near to removing the revelation entirely from actual life. His later writings on Christology are more emphatically on the side of the assertion that the Word of God is addressed to us through the real human being. Another example of the attempt to see history and revelation in right relation is afforded by Rudolph Bultmann's reconstruction of Paul's faith in which he sets forth the significance of Paul's statement that he is resolved to know Christ no more after the flesh. Paul is interested only in the fact that Christ became man and lived on earth. How he was born or lived interests him only to the extent of knowing that Jesus was a definite, concrete man, a Jew "being born in the likeness of man and being found in human form."[10] Bultmann interprets Paul's view of the incarnation, death and resurrection as "the eschatological salvation occurrence." That event is everywhere present as demand and as promise. "Lifted out of all temporal limitations, it continues to take place in any present moment both in the proclaiming word and in the sacraments."[11] But even if we grant that Bultmann is interpreting Paul correctly, when he further says "the personality of Jesus has no importance for the *kerygma* either of Paul or of John or for the New Testament in general,"[12] we wonder if he does justice to the full Christian faith. Why, we ask, did the Gospels record any of Jesus' doings and sayings? They tell of Jesus' attitude toward religious and ethical issues. He is crucified because he has drawn the enmity of religious and political groups upon himself. Whatever account we give of why Jesus died, we cannot leave out this historical circumstance. As John Bennett points out in his *Christian Realism,* a depreciation of the importance of the historical Jesus seems often accompanied by a depreciation of the prophetic element in his message.

We see that the attempt to relate the "two histories" to each other has its difficulties just as does the attempt to relate the "two natures." If the latter tradition seems to say, "There was a human nature, but it was not really concretely human in our sense," the new doctrine seems to say, "Jesus of Nazareth was truly a human historical person; but his history and personality do not matter in the revelation of the word of God." I have put these statements extremely to emphasize the issue involved.

So we are back at the problem of faith and history. We cannot have Christology without an answer to the question why it is that here in this particular history of Jesus and his community faith finds its proper object and its redemptive source. We must acknowledge the gain that is made when we see that faith cannot justify itself merely by pointing to some historical happenings. But it is about the relation between faith and these particular historical happenings that we have to try to be clear. It would be simpler to carry on the discussion from this point if we could say that this question has received an altogether satisfying answer in theology today. But it appears we shall have to accept the difficulty of this

problem; and say that the mystery of Christ yields no simple
clarity about Jesus as a historical person. In spite of the restiveness
of theology at this point, there is one lead which is opening up in
the Christological discussion in answer to the question how Jesus
and the Christ are together. To that we now turn.

III

An important advance in Christology today consists in the discovery of positive meaning just at the point where the tradition
seems in greatest difficulty. We have seen that modern historical
criticism emphasizes the humanity of Jesus of Nazareth, as a man
sharing a specific culture and tradition. It has further viewed the
New Testament as a faith document rather than as a strictly historical record. Finally, this criticism has left us with many uncertainties about the details of the history. In short, the finite character
of Jesus and of our knowledge of his life is stressed. Suppose now
that rather than regard this finite element as an embarrassment
to the Christian claim that God has spoken his decisive word in
Christ we see it *as intrinsic to the revelation itself*. Could we say
that the Christian faith claims final revelation in Christ just because
it gives us the picture of a finite person who acknowledges his own
limitation, and points beyond himself to God's truth which no
finite structure can fully express? If this thesis can be cogently
worked out, the reversal it brings to much traditional Christology
is startling. We would now rest the case for the ultimately decisive
character of the revelation in Christ, not upon miraculous signs
that the limitations of existence have been set aside, but upon the
discovery that there is a witness to God which comes through
those limitations. We still have to say why it is that the revelation
is given through Jesus. Not every finite person, but this One
becomes an adequate vehicle for the revelation. But we are saying
now that it is in the very humility of Jesus and his trusting accept-

ance of the risks and uncertainties of our human lot that we find not a barrier to God's word, but the very means for the communication of that Word.

This move to find new depth in the meaning of revelation through the results of historical criticism demands careful attention since the very possibility of Christian faith in relation to modern knowledge is involved. We shall consider how Paul Tillich, Reinhold Niebuhr, and H. N. Wieman work out this theme of disclosure through the finite in somewhat different theological contexts.

Paul Tillich's Christology is the central example and the crucial test of his theological method. Here he must show how the philosophical doctrine which sees finite existence in estrangement from the infinite God who is being itself, can be used to interpret the Biblical account of God's self-disclosure in the person, Jesus of Nazareth, who lived and died under the conditions of human existence. To assert that final revelation has been given in and through this historical life involves the profoundest problems of our understanding of human existence. It raises the question of how any such assertion is possible about an historical person whom we know only through the witness of those who wrote about him from the standpoint of faith. In dealing with the meaning of revelation in history, Tillich rarely refers to "Jesus" or to "the Christ," but usually to "the New Testament picture of Jesus as the Christ." In this way he both recognizes and passes beyond the difficulty of separating fact and interpretation in the Biblical record. The distinctive element in this Biblical "picture" is that Jesus points beyond himself to the Christ. "Jesus of Nazareth is the medium of the final revelation because he sacrifices himself completely to Jesus as the Christ." Tillich says a true perception of what is involved here means "the end of Jesusology" because the Christian faith must itself make this sacrifice if it is to understand its own revelation.[13] Tillich holds that only a revelation which involves the "breaking" of its own medium can be regarded as final without making intolerable claims to the absoluteness of some particular historical person or event. "A revelation is final if it has the power of negating itself without losing itself. . . . He who is the bearer of the final revelation must surrender his finitude—not only his life but his finite power and knowledge and perfection."[14] We see in Jesus the one who in the actual structure of human existence with all its limitations willed that through his life God's own work should be done. That will is love. It is the positive content of the revelation. We discover what God's love means only when we see it in a spirit which bears with our human condition, and opens the way to restoration of a trusting and loyal new life.

So far Tillich seems to have established a pattern for interpreting the meaning of revelation; but it may be asked, "Does not the Bible afford us the indispensable terms for understanding who Jesus was?" The Scripture calls him the Son of God, the Lord, the Saviour, the Logos become flesh. What can philosophy add?

It is just at this point that the full power of Tillich's method comes to the fore. What he does is to apply to the Biblical symbols themselves an analysis which shows that they have been transformed under the impact of the revelation in Christ so that we are free to appropriate their ultimate intent without being bound literally to historical versions of their meaning. The Bible itself shows us how the terms and categories used to interpret revelation, especially the revelation in Jesus, are "broken myths" which must be understood symbolically if we are to discern their real content. Yet each symbol has suffered the fate of being distorted anew when it has been formulated by a dogmatic and literal-minded authority. It is not possible to trace here Tillich's penetrating analysis of many Biblical terms such as Logos, Son of God, Lord. But the term "Christ" (Messiah) offers a decisive example. First developed as the symbol for expectation of divine intervention to redeem history from its evil, it was transformed under the impact of the crucifixion of Jesus. "A defeated Messiah is not a Messiah at all. Christianity acknowledges the paradox and accepts it."[15] Yet in the Christian vocabulary it is easy to distort the new meaning and to treat the Christ as a supernatural being who does not really share our humanity. The Christ bore the marks of finitude, even while he pointed through them to God.

The necessity of interpreting the incarnation in the light of the understanding of Jesus' humanity leads Tillich to a reappraisal of the orthodox formula of the union of two natures in the One Person. We must respect this traditional doctrine for it expressed in its time the two sides of the Christian assertion concerning the togetherness of God and man. It can be judged, however, as inadequate because "nature" in the Greek sense implies a static essence. Two such essences cannot be joined together to create one whole person. Hence Tillich proposes to substitute for the doctrine of the two natures the concept of "the unity of God and man" thus "replacing a static essence by a dynamic relation."[16]

What we know in Jesus Christ is the manifestation of the New Being in which existential estrangement has been faced and overcome. To participate in the new reality made manifest in Christ is to participate in the ultimate reconciliation of all estranged finitude with its absolute source in God, even while we continue to live on the earthly plane in the midst of the suffering and mystery of mortality.

The same theme is put by Dr. Reinhold Niebuhr in an ethical context. The religious problem of human history is how and when good will overcome evil. Historical injustice which stems from man's sinful pride is not adequately remedied in the course of history, nor is there any basis for believing that any immanent historical process will destroy the sources of evil. "How then can life have meaning?" Niebuhr asks. For him "meaning" in this religious sense depends upon confidence in the victory of the good. Christ comes as the answer. But he can be the answer only because he points beyond history to a resource which can overcome its contradictions. That resource is the suffering love of God. Niebuhr believes that Jesus, in order to point to God, must refuse to participate in the power struggles in history because self-interest corrupts all historical movements. "The significant contrast between the divine and the human in Christ is not, as Greek thought assumed, the contrast between the 'impassible and the passible.' It is a contrast between the perfect coincidence of power and goodness in the divine. It is impossible to symbolize the divine goodness in history in any other way than by complete powerlessness, or rather by a consistent refusal to use power in the rivalries of history."[17] Faith, then, points to the essential integrity with which Jesus disclosed the ultimate judgment and mercy which lie beyond history; but upon which the meaning of historical existence depends.

There are significant differences in H. N. Wieman's Christology from Niebuhr and Tillich. They differ on the relation of God to history. Wieman holds that unless God is an operative power at work redemptively in historical processes we cannot find hope or meaning. What lies "beyond history" does not really qualify what is in history. Wieman says that we must look for the basis of Christian faith at the actual operative relationship which Jesus sustained to his disciples. We must consider the effect upon them of his death with the experience of resurrection which followed. There came a release of the spirit in which God's redemptive power remade the lives of the believers.

Wieman's account of this redemptive release in *The Source of Human Good* has many points of agreement with the thesis of Niebuhr and Tillich in spite of their differences in the view of

God and history. It was Jesus' willingness to sacrifice all created goods, including his own wishes, meanings, plans, and his life itself to the "creative good of God," which opened the way to the new life for man. Jesus pointed away from himself as a personality enclosing the divine to the working of God which is continually breaking up old structures with the power of new life. The cross means for Wieman this reversal of human devotion from the good we now have to the good which God is giving. The life of the Christian becomes the "crucified life." It participates in the new relationship of commitment to God's new good which received its decisive disclosure through Jesus of Nazareth.

We cannot leave this problem without considering Professor Donald Baillie's constructive statement in *God Was in Christ*. Baillie has written one of the most original treatments of Christology in modern theology.

It is not clear, I think, just how far Baillie goes toward accepting the theme of Jesus as pointing beyond himself through his finite limitations. He tries to get at the mystery of the incarnation through reference to the paradox of grace in the Christian experience. What we accomplish in our human efforts depends upon what God gives. This is illustrated by the Christian conception of freedom. We are most free when we are doing the will of God. But in doing the will of God we are dependent upon God's power. Baillie believes this paradox cannot be rationalized; but it is the central truth of the Christian life.

Baillie's Christology rests upon his use of this paradox of grace to explain the incarnation. Jesus depends wholly upon God and gives his life up to God's service. Therefore, in him the grace of God is present in fullest measure. "His sinlessness consists in His renouncing all claim to ethical heroism. He did not set up at all as a man confronting God, but along with sinners—who do *not* take this attitude—He threw Himself solely on God's grace. The

God-Man is the only man who claims nothing for Himself, but all for God."[18] This seems to lay a similar stress to that of Tillich and Wieman on Jesus' giving up of all claims to what he possesses as Jesus to point to God.

The point on which Tillich's position relies, we have seen, is that Jesus can be the medium of revelation thus understood without requiring us to insist upon the "perfection" of the work of grace in him. But here the accent in Baillie's view seems to bring him back to a more traditional position. He appears to depend upon the "perfect union of God and man in the Incarnation." It is a union of grace and human nature "at the absolute degree." He states the problem of Christology thus: "We have to reckon with a life that was wholly human and wholly divine, neither side limiting the other at all."[19] If this means that God and Jesus are together in such a way that the revelation of forgiving love is adequate to our redemption, then all Christian faith will say as much. But if this denial of any limitations means that we have to affirm the traditional conception of an absolute perfection in a human life in order that it can be the medium of revelation, then Baillie's doctrine does stand more within the orthodox circle. How this latter view can be held together with an understanding of history which takes account of the real limitations of our knowledge is not clear. In his doctrine of paradox, Baillie himself seems to agree that this Christology will have to stand beyond any satisfactory rational formulation.

In all these Christologies we see an increasing concentration on that in the Christian faith which sees God coming to us through our humanity, not setting it aside. The love which saves is a love which bears with us. Through the broken windows of life the light comes through. This is not really a new theme, though modern historical understanding has sharpened it. The Bible has its own emphasis upon the strange humility of God. "There was no form or comeliness by which we might desire him," says the second Isaiah of the Suffering Servant. In the letter to the Philippians Paul sees the truth we are to make our own in Christ's taking upon himself the form of a slave. And there is the precious word of Jesus, "Why callest thou me good, there is none good but one, even God." The Protestant Reformers knew very well the doctrine that God's majesty is "hidden" as well as revealed in Christ. Luther says of Jesus on the cross, "There was He abased (Matt. xxvi,37) and made like a wretched, forsaken man in the presence *of God*. . . . He felt in his heart precisely as though He were deserted by God . . . the deity had secluded and concealed itself." Yet in this very abasement faith "sees the glory."[20]

Theology today is showing how Christian faith holds together its supreme claim that God's saving word is spoken in Christ with fidelity to the facts of our experience in a history which moves toward a future filled with mystery, but also with hope.

IV

In saying how God is present in Jesus Christ we are saying something about the nature of God. If he reveals himself through a life which bears human weakness in love, that must mean that God is bearing our plight. Does God himself suffer? There is a time-honored theological tradition which says he does not. But one of the most striking developments in theology today is the challenge to the doctrine of the "divine impassibility."

We miss what is involved in the question about God's suffering if we think primarily of physical pain, mental torment, or death. These are forms of human suffering, to be sure. In Christ God has in some way experienced them. But "suffering" has a broader meaning. It signifies to undergo, to be acted upon, to live in a give and take with others. To say that God suffers means that he is actively engaged in dealing with a history which is real to him.

What happens makes a difference to him. He wins an actual victory over the world through a love which endures and forgives. It means that the world's sorrow and agony are real for God, indeed in one way more real to him than to us, for only an infinite love can enter completely into sympathetic union with all life.

There are many lines of theological attack on the doctrine that God must remain completely impassive and unchanging through what takes place in history. We see in metaphysics, in Biblical theology, and in the theology of the Atonement three aspects of this structural shift in the Christian mind.

Charles Hartshorne, Edgar Brightman, F. R. Tennant, and A. N. Whitehead are among the Christian philosophers who have developed on rational and experiential grounds the meaning of God's suffering. Hartshorne has marshaled the tools of logical analysis to show that if God is intelligible to us at all he is unchanging in his essential nature; but changing in the content of his experience through his continual give and take with the world. We cannot here pursue the details of Hartshorne's argument. It will be found in his *Man's Vision of God* and *The Divine Relativity*. But we may point out that Hartshorne does not depend solely upon metaphysical analysis of time and the logic of relations for his thesis. He also argues persuasively that if we find some analogy to the divine love in our human experience, and if we cannot do so it is hard to see how there could be any knowledge of God, we know that love is a capacity to become responsive. Love which is not moved in any way by another is not strong; it is weak. For Hartshorne God must have an infinite capacity to receive as well as give for the very fulfillment of his love.

Biblical theology stresses God's dynamic relation to history. It has long been pointed out that the Hebrew consciousness of time as the realm of God's purposive action is quite different from the Greek understanding of time as the "moving image of eternity."

Oscar Cullmann, the Swiss New Testament scholar, has given a thoroughgoing analysis of what this means for the Biblical idea of God in his *Christ and Time*. Cullmann's thesis is that the Bible has no thought whatever of God's eternal being outside of time or apart from time. There is no eternity of rest before the creation; there is another time before this created world. There is no timeless age at the end of history. There is a new age. What this time of God before and after our earthly time means is, to be sure, only hinted in symbols. It defies adequate expression. But the Biblical account of God and the world declares God's temporal activity. He creates the world. History moves toward its midpoint in Jesus Christ. It moves on from the midpoint toward its end in resurrection and final judgment. This "end" is the beginning of the new life in God. In the work under discussion Cullmann does not discuss the effect of this interpretation upon the doctrine of the divine impassibility, or upon the question of whether all men are redeemed. But such an unequivocal statement of the "temporal" doctrine of God certainly appears to allow for more freedom, risk, and some real openness in the future.

The problem we are discussing comes to its sharpest focus in the doctrine of the Atonement. We might think that the death of Christ on the cross requires us to hold that there is suffering in God. But the tradition of "impassibility" says otherwise. Nels Ferré says, "The idea that the Father suffers with the Son is a heresy."[21]

Of course what we shall call heresy depends on our standard of orthodoxy; but it is true that theology has traditionally saved the impassibility of God by saying that on the cross only the human nature of Christ suffered. But the tendencies we have been examining in this chapter all lead in another direction. Suffering is not defeat when it comes from love and is sustained by love. Such suffering is the way love wins. Our human experience of love tells us that. A father does suffer with his son. How much more, then, does God's love achieve its deepest meeting with us, and its ultimate victory through God's suffering. He is not all suffering. He is power. He is inexhaustible creative energy. To say that God suffers does not take away from the majesty or the power of his love. It is rather the proof that his love has a strategy for dealing with evil.

This understanding that the cross is in God as well as in history finds theological expression in many different contexts. It may break with some orthodox tradition; but it releases a Christian insight. We have seen how Reinhold Niebuhr and Paul Tillich find the meaning of the salvation through the cross in that here we are brought to the acceptance of finitude, and trust in God is born in the midst of suffering. For Donald Baillie the atonement is eternally present in God. It becomes incarnate in the passion of Jesus. Baillie is willing to qualify the notion of impassibility. He accepts the theme of Gustaf Aulén's treatment of the atonement, *Christus Victor*, which is one of the most influential theological essays in recent years. Aulén says that the motif in which the Christian faith expresses most profoundly the meaning of atonement is that of God's warfare against evil and his winning of the victory through Christ. Traditionally this motif was expressed in mythical and even crude ways, such as Christ's death conceived as a ransom paid to the devil. But in Paul and in Luther the central thought is that God actively overcomes the evil powers in Christ. He does not wait for man to pay a debt which is owing him. While Aulén does not explicitly discuss the impassibility of God, this theory can hardly be conceived without a radical qualification of that doctrine.

Nicolas Berdyaev's theology shows how the emphasis of Christian existentialism upon God's personal encounter with man leads to a rejection of impassibility. Berdyaev is one of the most persuasive exponents of a Christian philosophy which combines mystical and existential elements. With an extraordinarily vivid style he defends the freedom of the human spirit against all institutionalism, dogmatism, and all powers which seek to confine man in some impersonal order of values. He gives expression to the theme of Christ's humiliation powerfully suggested in Dostoevski's novels and in a strong tradition in modern Russian orthodoxy. The humiliated Christ hangs on the cross to "draw men to himself." Only in this way can he save without destroying man's freedom. This truth that God saves through suffering alters our conception of the redeemed life which we symbolize by "paradise." Berdyaev says: "For Christian consciousness paradise is the Kingdom of Christ and is unthinkable apart from Christ. But this changes everything. The cross and the crucifixion enter into the bliss of paradise. The Son of God and the Son of Man descends into hell to free those who suffer there. . . . To conquer evil the good must crucify itself."[22]

Thus we see a powerful case being made today that love which does not come to its deepest knowledge and its redemptive power through suffering is not the love we know in Christ.

V

The Cross is set in paradise, according to Berdyaev. We come here to the question of "last things," eschatology. Where does it all come out? Are all saved? Who is saved? What does the end of history mean? We conclude this chapter by considering the bearing of the Christological discussion on these questions, for the way we see Christ in history determines what we see at the "end" of history.

The significance of eschatology took a central place in the discussions of the Assembly of the World Council of Churches in Evanston in 1954. The theme for the assembly was, "Jesus Christ as Lord, the only hope of both the church and the world." When the theological commission charged with drawing up a preliminary statement on the theme published its report, a vigorous discussion ensued in which certain topics such as "the second coming of Christ" took an increasingly important place.[23] Liberal Christianity has always been especially critical of doctrines stressing the return of Christ for fear they represent a willingness to relax the pressure to improve society as it is and encourage a fatalistic attitude toward the inevitable appearance of the Antichrist and the final conflict with evil. At the same time, the view so ably defended by Reinhold Niebuhr, that the Biblical eschatology in its main symbols is relevant to the understanding of history because it recognizes that there is no progressive triumph of good or evil, has been widely accepted. It could not be said that there emerged from Evanston any decisive agreement concerning how the Biblical and traditional eschatologies are to be understood in the light of modern knowledge. The question of how the Christian faith sees the trials and triumphs of history in relation to an ultimate judgment and fulfillment was sharply posed. We see that its implications cannot be avoided in any theology which is to be true to the Bible and to the perspective of the twentieth century, with its sense of history as the scene of conflict and the threat of destruction.

The issue here concerns what the Christian faith holds about how God saves the world. That his grace is present in history calling men to serve one another in love, and to create orders of justice, is not denied by any contemporary theology. The question is: What is it upon which the Christian faith rests its ultimate confidence? Does the promise of ultimate victory to which Christ's death and resurrection give witness, include a recognition of God's present power leading men toward a better order of life, though to be sure all historical achievements are fragmentary? Stated otherwise, does God redeem in part by what he accomplishes in the communities of achieved good in human existence, or solely by his creation of faith through Jesus Christ who will come again in glory? While the report obviously tries to include both emphases, it is noteworthy that it has little to say about the goodness of the creation as it comes from the hand of God or about his creative work in the world process. But there is widespread agreement, even from those who miss this emphasis, when the commission says: "From the standpoint of the gospel we must make clear that all human achievements are fragmentary, all responsibilities are subject to frustration, and all hopes based upon human power and wisdom alone are self-defeating." Therefore, we cannot avoid the eschatological question, filled as it is with mystery and insoluble problems.

The tendency we have been describing in Christology to stress the suffering of God as a real aspect of his dealing with history may lead to various interpretations of the ultimate outcome. Brightman and Wieman hold that God struggles in history, but that he may be thought of as winning a progressive victory there. Berdyaev seems to regard all world history as caught in the trap of impersonality. Only in a time which is beyond historical time does the truly saving revolution of the spirit take place. Some theologies hold with the more orthodox view that some men are really lost in a hardness of heart which eternity does not change. Ferré and Barth, on the other hand, seem to be turning to a universalist doctrine that in the end all are saved. Catholic orthodoxy, we have seen, denies that God suffers; but it has also held to the reality and eternity of hell for the damned. Generally one can notice a growing and commendable reticence in speculations concerning last things. What is more important is the view of history as moving from creation to judgment, with God's creative and redemptive grace actually entering into and qualifying all man's existence, and offering him ultimate hope. About this general perspective two points can be made.

First, there is renewed emphasis in theology today on the Biblical eschatology itself. The way in which the Bible sees human history and its outcome is expressed in the symbols of resurrection, Antichrist, last judgment, eternal life. Whatever differences there may be between the world view of Biblical times and ours, and whatever difficulties we may have in giving literal meaning to these concepts, they hold for us an understanding of what history is which is profoundly and eternally relevant to our actual experience. The New Testament sets God's creative act at the beginning of history, the cross in the midst of history, and God's judgment and mercy over all of history. There will always be differing Christian views as to the possibilities of human life in relation to God's suffering and forgiving love as it transforms our existence. But any simple utopian or smoothly progressive scheme of history cannot be reconciled with our Christian understanding that the dark mystery of sin leads God to the suffering of the Cross as the only way to bring man back to his high possibilities of life in community. Faith is guided in its expectations, then, by whatever understanding it can manage of resurrection, judgment, and eternal life. But the literal meaning of these final realities we cannot give. Some theologians simply interpret Biblical eschatological concepts according to their fundamental theological perspective, as Barth does, but make clear that we cannot give literal and detailed content to these "mysteries" which will only be clarified in the "last days." Others give meaning to the Biblical concepts by treating them as symbols which point to ultimate meanings which have relevance to our human experience of despair, crisis and hope. Tillich and Niebuhr deal in this way with the problem. Fundamentalist Christianity has an internal division between those who stress any of several "dispensationalist" views of history and those who believe that the Bible does not provide such a strictly defined pattern for the action of God in history.[24] Those who hold to the literal interpretation of Scripture, as well as those who seek to reinterpret the Biblical symbols, may agree that the Christian faith affirms the limits of our knowledge concerning the future and concerning the mode of God's judgment and final fulfillment of the achievements and tragedies of historical existence.

Also rejected almost universally in Christian theology is the notion that since faith expects a final intervention of God, there is nothing to be done constructively in history but to save individual souls and wait passively for the end. We are called to serve in whatever responsible roles God opens up to us in life. Love always reaches out to the neighbor in justice and mercy.

The second point has to do with the question raised for the Evanston conference of the limitations placed by Christian thought on what is to be expected of constructive action toward a better order of life. Here a wide difference seems to appear in the Christian mind. Without overlooking the depth of the issue, I believe we can cautiously state a principle which might be accepted by all sides as we try to find our way through this problem. The principle is that we can never put such restriction on God's work of grace in history as to deny the real new life which he gives through his creative and redemptive action culminating in Jesus Christ. We must never deny that God has in the very creation itself expressed the holy and vital order of a community of good. That is what creation through the *logos* means. And we cannot deny that when the *logos* becomes flesh the way is opened for men here and now to enter into a new relationship to God in which his Holy Spirit frees us for a reconciled and released way of love. It is true that our participation in Christ is partly anticipation of the promise of fulfillment. The "eschatological view of Christ" means we live by a foretaste of life in glory, not the possession of it. But it is a real participation. "If any man be in Christ, he is a new creation," says Paul. That is a statement about what can be here and now. Christ's death and resurrection point forward, but what they point to is given its foundation already in him. On that foundation, within the limits of our weakness, an order of life can come which fulfills in some measure God's will for his creatures. In his *Faith and History* Reinhold Niebuhr has reiterated his conviction that renewals of the spirit and of culture are possible in history. In spite of its "pessimistic tone" the report of the World Council commission said plainly, "Every effort to support man's rightful hopes, every act of neighborly forbearance and self-giving, every experience of reconciliation and every achievement of genuine community in the Christian's encounter with his fellow men, is an act of obedience to God's will in Christ and a token of the cross and the final triumph of Christ."

It remains to point out that whatever Christian hopes we have for real victory of God in history are related to our knowledge that in Christ God shows how suffering is involved in the strategy of redemptive love. If we see love's suffering, not as defeat, but as a movement within the work of forgiveness and mercy, exposing the evil and releasing the good, then we know why the Christian faith is so filled with hope in the midst of a humanity no stranger to suffering.

We may express the theme of this chapter by reference to two well-known paintings of Christ. A modern painting exhibited at the Century of Progress exhibition in 1933 is entitled, "The Triumphant Christ." Its Christ is a religious hero, surveying with flashing eye the world he has conquered. He is filled with vital power and the glow of victory achieved. The other painting is Grünewald's "Crucifixion" with its lonely Christ hanging on the cross as John the Baptist points a bony finger toward him. The face of Christ is distorted in the agony of the thorns upon his head and the nails which fix him to the cross. All the suffering in the world is gathered into the features twisted with pain and sorrow.

The artist who drew the triumphant Christ had an authentic word to say about the meaning of the Gospel. But while Grünewald's Christ is dark with suffering, is he not also far more eloquent of that hope which love alone understands?

POSTSCRIPT TO CHAPTER V

In order to keep continuity in the present chapter, I have followed the theme of the suffering God and its implications for Christology, especially as found in recent Protestant theology. In doing this I have passed by what is surely one of the most impressive achievements in Christological thought, that in the Anglican communion.

Some modern Anglican theology shows considerable sympathy with the trends we have described. From Gore to Temple the more "liberal" theologians have sought to stress the real humanity of Jesus, always within the framework of the creeds, but with radical qualifications of traditional supernaturalism. The one point we can make here is that especially in the Anglo-Catholic group today there is a stricter adherence to the supernatural interpretation of Chalcedonian orthodoxy. In a public lecture Canon Leonard Hodgson stated that the problem of Christology is to say how Jesus of Nazareth had both a truly human mind and the divine mind.[25] Hodgson stated his dissatisfaction with all the modern attempts at a solution. But if I understand the import of this formulation, it means that in spite of modern historical understanding we are still within the framework of a metaphysical supernaturalism. God's mind must be somehow joined to a human mind. What Hodgson seems to suggest is certainly carried out in two recent works by Anglo-Catholics.

In *The Incarnate Lord* Father L. S. Thornton shows how the understanding of Christ can be brought into unity with the theme of emergent evolution, especially as developed in Whitehead's philosophy. Each new level of being increases in complexity, in freedom, in individuality and social relationships. Each new level incorporates all previous levels. The incarnation appears in one sense as the culmination of the process at the highest level. The incarnate Lord incorporates the structure of the whole creation; but he does it in that new order of being which is his own person. The incarnation does not then simply emerge from below: God comes down to crown the whole process through his revelation of its ultimate source. Thornton brilliantly maintains here the Anglican theological method of synthesis of rational metaphysics with a superrational doctrine of revelation. But if Jesus Christ is a new order of existence, transcending the human order, it is difficult to see how he is truly man. Donald Baillie raises this question about his finely balanced *Christ in the Christian Faith*. Dr. Pittenger's full Christology is given in his *The Word Incarnate* which is the first thorough interpretation of the Christological themes in the light of the process doctrines of Whitehead and Hartshorne.

E. L. Mascall stands closer to the Thomist metaphysics than to Whitehead's. He wants to reconcile "a real omniscience in our Lord's human nature with an equally real growth and development."[26] This is accomplished by the theory that Jesus' omniscience was precisely adjusted in each instant to the requirements of the immediate situation. But again we have to ask whether we are any longer talking about a real human mind.

CHAPTER VI

The Church

THROUGH the preaching of the gospel of God's redemptive action in Jesus Christ a new people comes into being in history, the Church. Theology arises within this new community, is addressed to it, and has as one of its major tasks the interpretation of its form and spirit.

We shall not here direct our attention to the discussions between the different branches of the Church concerning the possible basis of reunion. These ecumenical discussions are important and extensive. Much theological labor is going into the attempt to achieve mutual understanding in matters of authority, the sacraments, the ministry, and other aspects of the form of the Church. It would be impossible in this one chapter to review that whole discussion. I propose rather to point out that there is another movement in Christian thought about the Church today, which will continue to go on whatever happens in these ecumenical conversations. This movement is an "internal reformation" within the existing denominations which is producing structural changes in most of the churches of Christendom. Within nearly every existing Christian communion there is a growing challenge to complacency with the existing forms and traditions. Each communion is actually only a fragment of what the full Body of Christ should be. The question being asked from within the churches is, "How can the universal Church of Christ be more adequately expressed in our particular tradition?" This internal reformation of the Church takes as its presupposition what the present Archbishop of Canterbury has said, "No age of the Church, no school of theologians, no single Church, has ever comprehended the 'wholeness' of the Christian faith without any falsity of emphasis or insight."[1] This opens the way for a radical self-criticism on the part of every existing church. The theological expressions of this self-criticism which we discuss in this chapter probably represent a minority voice even among the theologians in many instances. A leader of the American Congregationalists recently described the graduates of Congregational seminaries today as "High Church Congregationalists," a term which may not apply to the majority of ministers or laity in this communion. And the liturgical movement in the Roman Catholic Church with its "protestantizing" tendencies is certainly led by a small and embattled group, yet it appears to be one of the most creative movements in that Church. Dr. Arthur E. Holt once remarked, "Society rarely advances majority end foremost." The same is true of the churches.

In order to judge the significance of this self-criticism within the existing Christian denominations we need to remember two facts about the situation of the Church in the world today. The first is that many divisions among the Christian communions are going to persist. Great as are the strides toward church unity in an ecumenical life which breaks down old barriers, there is still a mountain of inherited differences of faith, form and spirit to be moved. Every move of one group toward union with another tends to produce a strong counterreaction within that church. Further, the closer one church moves toward another the farther it may find itself from a third. If Episcopalians move toward union with Presbyterians they create a deeper cleavage with those who would move toward the Orthodox Church or toward Rome. For a long time to come we shall have to live within a divided Christendom. In fact, the ideal of one household of faith does not rule out diversity of form and practice. Therefore, what is happening within the existing forms to increase the full ministry of the Church to men is of utmost importance. We could say that ecumenicity has two dimensions, one external, the other internal. The first has to do with uniting different communions and traditions in a fuller common life. Internal ecumenicity means the discovery of the fuller life in the Body of Christ through renewal and reformation within existing churches. Both movements are necessary.

The second fact which makes this internal ecumenicity of crucial importance today is that the Church's capacity to offer itself as the community of faith, transcending all the lines of division which cut life to pieces, is one of its major evangelistic opportunities. Any analysis of what people are seeking uncovers the deep human need to find the group to which one belongs, and in which he finds reinforcement and recognition. The anxiety of "nonbelonging" is perhaps the deepest of all human anxieties. But the individual does not really want that to which he belongs to destroy either his freedom or his security. Hence neither individualism nor totalitarianism can satisfy the human spirit. Desperate men swing to one extreme or the other. They will surrender their freedom to the totalitarian state for a promised security. Desperate individualists will resist all collective restraints, but give up the hope which comes from acknowledging that one's own life can only be fulfilled in a community of mutual understanding and love. The Christian Church in essence is the one universal community which answers to the deepest need of men. It is not a substitute for family, nation, trade union or club. But it differs from all of these because it relates men to eternal destiny and holds up the one loyalty to God above all other loyalties. The community of the Church unites personal freedom and a shared life in one social organism. It offers the kind of human relationships which are appropriate to sinners who are reconciled to one another through God's grace. It is just this community of reconciliation and eternal life which no secular order by itself can bestow. The profound tension in human relations between individualism and collectivism is met within the Church, and finds the foundation for its solution there. If in faith we hold this to be true, then the Church as the "new people among the people" can bear in its own life a practical witness to hope for a new, decent and peaceful order for the peoples of the world. In spite of manifest failures, the churches show signs of a renewal from within to achieve a more adequate demonstration of this possibility.

I

The internal movement in the Church today can be described by saying that "Protestant" churches are emphasizing that they really share in the catholic character of the Body of Christ; and the "Catholic" churches are finding that they must emphasize aspects of faith and worship for which Protestantism stands. These terms "catholic" and "protestant" give us increasing trouble just because from both sides there is a growing will to include what is important in the other. We ordinarily use the term "Catholic" to refer to the Roman, Eastern Orthodox, and, in part, the Anglican tradition. We use the term "Protestant" often quite indiscriminately for all other churches. The increasing dissatisfaction with this usage is a symbol of the movement we are describing. Who is catholic, and who is protestant?

To answer that question we have to recall that the word "catholic" as it is used in the Apostles' Creed—"I believe in the holy catholic church"—means universal, integral and whole. The catholic church then is the one which realizes in its own life the universal structure and the whole life of the community of believers in Christ. In this sense the "Protestant" churches are increasingly asserting their "catholicism." We shall see now what this emphasis means, and some practical implications it has for the worship and life of Protestants.

A group of British Free Churchmen has recently prepared a statement with the significant title "The Catholicity of Protestantism" in response to some questions from the Archbishop of Canterbury. They seek to go behind the excessive individualism of nineteenth-century tendencies which obscured the nature of the Church and to get back to the Church as understood at the origin of Protestanism in the Reformation. With an impressive body of scholarship they say, "No one who is acquainted with the writings of Luther or Calvin, or indeed any of the great sixteenth century Reformers, could deny that they possessed the catholic Faith and the other elements necessary for 'wholeness.' "[2] The original and fundamental Protestant teaching on the Bible, the sacraments, the grace of God, all come within the properly catholic understanding of the objective and corporate nature of the forms through which God's grace is given to the Church and the individual. The authors find their greatest difference with the "Catholic" theologies at the point of understanding the freedom and universal efficacy of the Holy Spirit in the Church. Protestant theology rejects the binding of the spirit to forms and institutions in any exclusive way, and therefore must assert that the Holy Spirit has been effectively present wherever the word of God has been preached and heard, and wherever faith has arisen in active personal response to the word.

In his book *The Nature of Catholicity* the British Congregationalist Daniel Jenkins undertakes an even more systematic analysis of what is necessary to "catholicity." He asserts that the foundation of the Church is Jesus Christ, the word of God as the Bible bears witness to the word. The Bible is the Church's book but it holds before the Church that which stands above it in judgment and in mercy, God's redemptive grace. The wholeness or catholicity of the Church then means its fidelity to God's present, active and demanding word in Jesus Christ. Whatever gives adequate expression and corporate life in a social body to the reality of this word is "catholic." In his later *Tradition and the Spirit* Jenkins has gone on to show how Protestantism can and must acknowledge the way in which "tradition" functions in the communication and preservation of its witness to the word of God. We see Protestant theology today trying to assert its own deeper essence. It is making as explicit as possible the truth of the ancient maxim that Christ and the Church belong together. This theological movement gives an answer to the standing charge that "Protestants do not take the Church seriously." This charge does not have to do with superfical matters. Of course Protestants have churches, congregations and denominations. The question is, do Protestants understand that this "new people among the people" is an organic part of God's redemptive work, that the Church is a bearer of grace to the individual and in some sense for him? The emphasis on catholicity we are describing meets this charge head on by showing that the proper Protestant understanding of the work of grace does take the Church seriously as the actual society through which God's redemptive grace normally moves. The point of this renewed emphasis can be made in relation to Schleiermacher's dictum that Catholicism makes the individual's relationship to Christ dependent on his relationship to the Church, and Protestantism makes the individual's relationship to the Church dependent upon his relationship to Christ. Schleiermacher, it should be noted, feared the excessive individualistic emphasis and said that this distinction was "provisional." Most Protestant theology in the modern period of ecumenical churchmanship would insist that either extreme is a violation of the true nature of the Church. To be in Christ is to be in the Church. They are interdependent. Of course Church here does not mean simply an institution and its formal boundaries of membership. It means the corporate body of believers. God's word in Christ saves us just by bringing us within such a body where life is shared, sustained and renewed in a loving relationship to others. Christ is the one head of this new people which is in its essence catholic, that is, "universal and whole."

One reflection of this Protestant understanding of the Church is found in the way Protestant scholars are looking at the New Testament record of the origins of the Church. Every Christian group tends to find its own understanding of the Church supported by the New Testament. Individualistic Protestants sometimes argued that Jesus never founded a church at all. Catholics have claimed that their views of authority, episcopacy and other matters are almost universally supported by the early Church. Against both it is safe to say we will never have absolutely final answers on the question of Jesus' intention or the form of the Church in New Testament times. But Protestant scholars are prominent among those today who assert the central place which the Church holds both in Jesus' message and in the earliest preaching of the gospel. There is weighty reason for believing that Jesus' preaching of the coming of the Kingdom included his preparation of the little group of believers as the new congregation, the "ecclesia" as the people of the new covenant. R. Newton Flew says, "the new community, even in the present age, is clearly envisaged by our Lord. It is the "little flock" to which it is the good pleasure of His Father to give the *Basileia*" (Kingdom).[3] In his reconstruction of the first Christian preaching, C. H. Dodd shows that the Gospel message from the beginning contained an announcement of Christ's reign as the Messianic head of the New Israel; affirmed the presence of the Holy Spirit in the Church as the sign of his reign, and offered forgiveness and the promise of salvation to all who enter the elect community. The phrase which Dodd uses, the "New Israel," does not appear, it is true, in the New Testament, though Paul does speak once of the Christian community as the "Israel of God." But the essential point is that from the beginning the Christian Gospel interpreted the action of God's redemptive word in Christ as creating a new people out of those who were not yet a people because they had not obtained mercy, as the First Epistle of Peter expresses it. Dr. C. C. Morrison in his *What Is Christianity* has stressed both on Biblical and theological grounds the continuity of the community of the old covenant with that of the new covenant in which Christ has broken through all national and cultural boundaries. Here the theologian of the Protestant Disciples of Christ gives an argument in many respects parallel to that of the Anglo-Catholic Lionel Thornton in his *The Common Life in the Body of Christ.* Thus Protestants and Catholics alike declare the integral place of the Church in the Gospel. Even the words recorded in Matthew 16:17-19 as being spoken by Jesus to Peter, "thou art Peter, and upon this rock I will build my church," which for a long time were looked at with gravest suspicion by Protestant scholars as not authentic, are now regarded in a somewhat different light. Karl Schmidt and others are inclined to accept them as authentic.[4] They are Jesus' assertion that preparation for the new age of the reign of God involves entry into the community which was to come into being through the preaching of Peter and the other disciples. Acceptance of this interpretation would still leave open the question of the kind of authority which Jesus intended the Church to possess if the further words, "Whatsoever thou shalt bind on earth shall be bound in heaven: and whatsoever thou shalt loose on earth shall be loosed in heaven," are also to be regarded as his own. Flew says there is no necessity for regarding that authority in a legalistic manner.

Before we go on to consider the implications of this catholic emphasis in Protestantism we need to ask briefly whether there is anything distinctive about a Protestant doctrine of the Church. A formula suggested by Paul Tillich opens the way to an answer. Tillich says the true Christian direction in understanding the Church is to affirm its catholic substance together with the prot-

estant principle. The catholic substance is the historically given
witness to the revelation in Bible, Creeds, church order, Sacraments and devotional life. The protestant principle can be understood in relation to Tillich's Christology which we discussed in the
preceding chapter. God saves us by exposing the limitations of all
historical forms and values. The protestant principle means the
acknowledgment of God's judgment which stands above all finite
truth, forms, symbols and institutions. The Church itself is under
the judgment of the Gospel which it proclaims. This means that
all earthly authority is qualified. Not even the most sacred forms
in which the Church expresses its faith can be regarded as
guaranteeing in themselves that they are in every situation bearers
of God's grace. All are subject to the protest which comes in the
name of the God whose spirit is free above all forms.[5] Walter
Marshall Horton once described the Church as Protestants understand it as "a frequently purged and sifted community." A radical
application of the protestant principle does not mean abolition of
form and tradition but a continual openness to reformation in the
light of fresh encounter with God's word and Spirit. It is certainly
not the case that historically all Protestant churches have either
accepted or honored this protestant principle. Granting of absolute
authority to particular historical forms or persons has been evident
in Protestantism perhaps as much as in the Catholic traditions.
But many Protestants today hold that this is because the true
meaning of "justification by faith" as over against dependence
upon sacred forms has yet to be fully realized in Protestantism.
We never have God's grace apart from some historical form. In
the Christian Church with its Bible, Creeds, preaching and
Ministry we have Christ's very Body in history; yet the Bible itself
makes clear we may have the form without the spirit. The Head
is above the Body, in the Christian analogy. "Why call ye me
Lord, Lord, and do not the things which I say?"

One expression of the intensified consciousness of the catholic elements in the Church is that Protestantism is experiencing its own liturgical revival. We in America are familiar with one striking evidence of this in the rebuilding of countless auditorium type churches with center pulpits so as to place altar or communion table and the cross in the place of central attention. This trend is sometimes regarded as an aesthetic fashion lacking the support of theological understanding. There is something in this judgment; but it appears to me superficial. What congregations are seeking is the way in which the Church through its place of worship can manifest its apprehension of the abiding realities which create and sustain it.

The Protestant problem is to interpret sacramental worship, the nature of preaching, and the place of the Bible in the corporate life in such a way that the freedom of the spirit which the protestant principle demands is preserved. Here theology has found a resource in going back to the Reformation period and recovering the fundamental intent of Protestant worship. We have quoted the authors of *The Catholicity of Protestantism* in their appreciation of the essentially catholic outlook of Luther and Calvin. Two other recent works have stressed the high churchmanship which went into the reconstruction of worship in the first Lutheran and Reformed churches. The Swedish scholar Yngve Brilioth in his *Eucharistic Faith and Practice* shows the central place of the sacrament in Luther's teaching as one form of proclamation of God's word which creates and sustains the new fellowship in Christ.

Brilioth's book was published in 1926 and remains one of the major studies of Christian worship. He says that his understanding of the tradition of his own Church of Sweden was helped more than anything else by his experience of the "fuller sacramental life of the English Church," another example of the stimulus of ecumenical encounter.[6] Brilioth's constructive analysis of the communion into thanksgiving, communion-fellowship, commemoration, sacrifice, including the act of memorial and the Church's self-oblation, and "mystery" which "embraces and unites all the others," has influenced much recent Protestant interpretation of worship.[7]

What Brilioth does for the Lutheran tradition, H. D. Davies has done for Calvinism in *The Worship of the English Puritans*. He traces the reconstruction of the Mass worked out by Bucer and later by Calvin at Strassburg. Calvin's original intent was to have the Christian service of worship offer the word of God both in the form of preaching and the communion each Sunday. When the Genevan magistrates forbade such frequent celebration, the preparation for the communion and the preached word remained, and only the actual celebration of the sacrament was omitted.

In some free churches the Lord's Supper has become only an occasional observance, and its meaning has tended to be lost in obscurity or reduced to superficial dimensions. Today there is a renewal of attention to the central place which the sacrament holds as a presentation of the full word of God in Christ to the congregation and within its corporate life. Celebration of the Lord's Supper is an act of the whole Christian body in new encounter with God's eternal word. It is not merely a remembrance of things past; it is a memorial, a present recreation of the relationship between man and God in which we are bound together anew in Christ's grace and in his service.

The problem of Protestant sacramentalism is to keep the freedom of the spirit under the protestant principle. It is Jesus Christ who is proclaimed in the communion service. His grace can only be received in the personal faith of the participant. Without faith, no real sacrament. But a more corporate Protestant understanding of the Church can hold firmly to this principle and still allow that the faith of the Christian exists in mutual dependence with the faith of the other members of the Christian body. In this sense the sacrament not only comes to the individual with the reinforcement of the faith of all Christians but it is itself a celebration of that solidarity. It can further be said that from a Protestant point of view, the forms of celebration of the sacrament cannot be treated as inflexible and as binding the freedom of the Holy Spirit. The signs and seals of Christ's sacrifice have been shared efficaciously with multitudes of Christians under diverse forms and many ecclesiastical administrations.

Preaching is one of the two forms in which the word of God is offered to the Christian congregation in the Protestant view. A liturgist of the Episcopal Church once remarked to the writer that in the present liturgical revival one could bring together scholars from nearly every communion, and they would agree on the essential elements and requirements for Christian worship. This is true, I believe, with one exception, that is preaching. The Catholic churches tend to regard preaching as primarily instruction, or inspiration, or in certain circumstances, evangelism. But the Protestant faith is that preaching is always one form of offering the word of God. We have seen in Karl Barth's theology how the preached word stands along with Jesus Christ and with the Bible, though dependent upon them. To be sure, much Protestant interpretation of preaching has not put the matter this way. But what is involved is the sacramental character of preaching, and upon this there is new emphasis at the present time.

In a book on preaching entitled *The Servant of the Word,* H. H. Farmer has stressed the personal relationship in the encounter between God and Man. He interprets the event of preaching as one way in which the encounter may take place. This interpretation relieves the preacher of some burdens, but places upon him the highest responsibilities. It releases him from the illusion that the vital thing is his own opinions, or his skill in producing emotional response. Of course his ability in interpretation and communication is necessary. But the center of attention is upon that for which the minister himself is listening in his preparation and his utterance, when he is given the grace to listen, that is God's word of judgment and reconcilation for this man and this congregation here and now.

The Bible's place in the Church is not exclusively related to preaching. The Bible is the Holy Book of a people. It came out of the long history of a community of faith. It has always served in Protestantism as a living guide to the progress of the pilgrim, the statesman, the nation builder, and the proclaimer of the Christian way. While today the Bible has become virtually a closed book for many Christians, this conception of preaching as opening up the truth which the Bible contains for the congregation, and the renewed theological emphasis on the Bible as giving the structural foundation for all Christian thinking, are leading toward a widespread re-education of the Church in a critical understanding of the Biblical record. The publication of several new translations, and such complete new commentaries as *The Interpreter's Bible,* reflect the new Biblical consciousness. Under the protestant principle a critical understanding of the Bible is essential if the Church is to be kept free from serving a new idol in the literal word of a book rather than in the truth which it expresses through human and limited means. The so-called life-situation preaching which was characteristic of liberal Protestantism has been subjected to some perhaps justified criticism as not having been sufficiently grounded in the Bibical perspective. But the truth the Bible holds must be brought into personal encounter with the life situation of the hearer if preaching is to succeed at all in its purpose. A Biblical preaching which is at the same time genuinely contemporary with our time and problems is not easy to achieve; but no Christian preaching can intend to be any less.

We see then a centering down in Protestantism toward a more catholic consciousness of the Church, a deeper appreciation of the historical roots of Protestantism in thought which was at once catholic and informed by a radical interpretation of the meaning of Christian freedom. The protestant spirit will never set limits to God's free exercise of his sovereignty and saving grace.

II

The churches ordinarily called "Catholic" do not need perhaps to plead their adherence to the conception of the whole and universal Body of Christ as the mediating society of grace. They have always held the doctrine of the Church to be an elaboration of the "structure of the divine society," to use Professor Dillistone's phrase. Yet on the Catholic side also there is now a recognition that no existing communion is truly "whole." The late William Temple expressed the point in a characteristically generous way when he stated his ideal for his own Anglican communion:

> If a man sets out to be loyal to the Catholic tradition, so understood as to rule out all that is distinctive of the Reformation, he cannot also be fully loyal to the Church of England. If a man sets out to be loyal to the Reformation, so understood as to rule out any elements of the Catholic tradition which were not universally maintained by the Reformed Churches, he cannot also be loyal to the Church of England. The Church of England has always bridged the gulf (or sat on the hedge, if you like) that divides "Catholic" and "Protestant" from one another.[8]

One important movement of the Roman Catholic and other churches toward one another is in the form and interpretation of Christian worship.[9] The far-reaching changes adopted by the Second

Vatican Council in such matters as the use of the vernacular in the celebration of the Mass, the re-ordering of the celebration so that the priest faces the people as he stands behind the table placed in front of the altar or in the center of the congregation, the stress upon lay participation, and the celebration of the sacrament as the act of the whole body of Christ, are all the fruit of a vital liturgical movement which has been doing solid work and gathering strength for many years. Protestant and Catholic liturgists have been in direct and fruitful discussion with one another, especially in Germany. There are many Protestant counterparts as in the Taizé community in France.

Beyond these practices which stress the Mass as collective action there is the more important matter of the theological interpretation of the relation of the congregation to what is happening in the liturgy. Roman Catholic theology has a place for the doctrine of the "priesthood of all believers"; but the leaders of the liturgical movement have made more explicit than before what its implications are for the Mass. It means that the priest does not act simply for the believers, but that they are all together acting through him. In these ways the movement seeks the cultivation of explicit faith and understanding on the part of the Catholic worshiper, as over against reliance only upon the implicit faith which he has vicariously through the Church as a whole. Non-Roman Christians can certainly regard this as a direction with which they are in full sympathy. Authentic ecumenical worship has become a reality.

Even more fundamental new directions have to do with the interpretations of the sacrament itself. The *Mystery Theology* which has given theological foundations to the liturgical movement interprets the symbols in the Christian sacraments as efficacious signs of the "mysteries" of the faith, that is, of the spiritual reality and effects of Christ's life and death. There is no denial of the Real Presence of Christ in the Sacrament; but the nature of his presence would appear to be that which involves the relation between an eternal reality and the symbol of action which is its historical expression, that is, the communion meal. The point involved is subtle and one who looks at it from the outside may easily misunderstand; but it is hard to escape the impression that this way of looking at the Mass makes the whole more intelligible by freeing it from the crass materialism which so easily becomes a kind of magic. The theory appears to have more affinity with the Augustinian conception of grace as spirit infused into nature than it does with the Thomist theory of grace as transforming substantively the sacramental bread and wine. Further, if spiritual things are spiritually received then the mysteries which are presented in the Mass would appear to have most meaning when they are consciously understood and appropriated by the believer.

The close connection between the liturgical movement and the Catholic Action movements which have shown such constructive pioneering in evangelization especially in France, comes from the same emphasis on the participation of Christians in the Mystical Body of Christ, and on the liturgy as the Church's first means of teaching what Christianity is.

The address of Pope Paul VI at the National Eucharistic Congress in Pisa on June 10, 1965 appeared to put definite restraint on the tendency of the Mystery Theology. He reaffirmed the real presence of Christ in the sacrament in terms which apparently repeat the literal formula of transubstantiation, the transformation of the substance of the elements into the body and blood of Christ. He spoke of "this real and hidden presence under signs deprived of their real nature (bread and wine), but filled with the specific significance of the Eucharist (spiritual food for man on the way to life eternal). The elements "contain the living and true Christ." [10]

There can be no question, however, of the radical character of the new interpretation of the nature of the Church and the structure of authority within the Church. Hans Küng in a review of the Second Vatican Council has stressed the genuinely new position of the Church on many matters. He says, "The Pope is not an absolute monarch. Without prejudice to his primacy, it is stated in the Constitution of the Church that the bishops, together with the Pope have a common, *collegial* responsibility for the Church." [11]

Vatican II is one of the great events in Christian history, and is both the result and the opening of the way to a creative theological advance. Now every aspect of the Christian Faith will be examined in an ecumenical dialogue with a new freedom.

III

The standing Protestant criticism of Anglican theologians is that though they are heirs of the Reformation, they do not take it seriously. Of first importance, therefore, is the thesis set forth by the Anglican Frederick W. Dillistone, in *The Structure of the Divine Society*. He gets at the most fundamental questions which have divided Christians by showing that the Church has been understood mainly on the basis of two different conceptions which have existed in tension and conflict. The "organic" and the "covenantal" relations have offered the two most important structural analogies for defining the Church. The organic conception has its basis and its validity in the fact that we are members of a social body. We are born into family and nation and receive from such given relationships the very possibility of personal identity and worth. The covenantal relations are those into which we enter voluntarily through personal commitments to one another as we look toward some common purpose for the future. In the human family we have a relationship in which these two principles are held creatively together.[12] Dillistone shows that theology has interpreted man's relationship to God through these two types of structure. He believes both are valid and that the Christian Church can incorporate and reconcile them. Catholicism has generally stressed the organic doctrine. Protestants have stressed the aspects of personal freedom and commitment in the covenantal theory. Here Dillistone, the Anglican, acutely interprets the Church theory of the Puritans. A widespread acceptance of this analysis would make it impossible for any Christian denomination to remain satisfied with its present self-interpretation.

When we turn to the Anglo-Catholic Group we find theology stressing the organic theory. The Church is the divine society, one living supernatural organism, deriving from the original community of Israel, and now transformed through Jesus Christ. It moves through history as the grace-filled Body of Christ, continually incorporating new life through its sacramental action which takes the common life up into itself where it is transfigured in the light of grace. Father A. G. Hebert, Michael Ramsey, Lionel Thornton and others have elaborated this doctrine. The Church is defined according to an interpretation of the apostolic and New Testament message which holds Bible, Creeds, Sacraments and Ministry, conceived within the office of the Episcopate, to constitute its essential form.

In a sense this Anglo-Catholic ecclesiology, which is being stated today with vast Biblical and historical scholarship, may not seem to be moving any closer to a recognition of the characteristic emphasis of the covenantal type on freedom of the spirit. But the Anglo-Catholics are a reforming party within their own communion with respect to liturgy, social action and doctrine. At many points that reformation is opening the way to rethinking of old problems so that the Catholic doctrine of the Church is being put in a new light.

The Anglo-Catholic liturgical movement is reinterpreting the

Church's sacramental life. There are striking developments in the move to revise the liturgy in the direction of simplicity, personal participation of the worshipers, and above all a centering of attention on the essential meaning of the Church's worship. An outstanding work is that of Dom Gregory Dix, *The Shape of the Liturgy*. He analyzes the classic form of the eucharistic action which, the Church holds, was instituted by Christ. The four elements are: First, *the offertory*. Originally the bread and wine and other gifts were brought by the congregation to be blessed, consecrated and distributed. Second, the *prayer*, which is at once the blessing and the thanksgiving. Third, the *fraction*. The original breaking of the bread for distribution is taken up into the Christian memorial of the passion of Christ. Fourth, the *communion* as the believers partake of the elements. Dix argues that what is needed is a true perception and acknowledgment of what the eucharistic action is, divested of many ritual encumbrances and of theological wanderings from its central theme. His own approach to the reconstruction of the liturgy is informed by an appreciation of creative freedom. He says the great liturgy must grow. There is no solution through adopting the forms of a past century or trying to repristinate primitive Christian practice. But there is no doubt that his proposals would lie in the direction of a disciplined effort to have the sacramental action and words express with directness and a certain austerity the saving action of God in the life, death and resurrection of Jesus Christ. Dix supports the contention which we have seen even some Roman liturgical reformers making that a wrong turn was taken in the medieval period with the separation of the Mass from the people. It lost its character as the action of the whole Church which is the "very core of Christian practice."[13] This stripping off of the weight of historical accumulation in the determination to get at the essentials of Christian worship can lead to the breaking of new ground in whatever Christian group it may take place.

The recent discussion of baptism by the Anglicans has raised some interesting questions. Baptism has always been a special problem in Christianity, particularly in the case of infants. Of course some groups have rejected infant baptism. Those churches which have practiced it, especially the politically established ones, have become acutely conscious of the scandal of providing this Christian ceremony for all and sundry regardless of real Christian profession or intention. A commission of the Church of England has recently studied the problem. It finds a special difficulty in the long period between baptism and confirmation, which leaves many years in which growing youths are denied the communion, very often have no Christian instruction, and perhaps are never confirmed at all. Some measures toward strengthening the process by which baptism in infancy may be followed by normal growth in the Christian life are proposed, but the underlying question of the significance of baptism for the infant remains a perplexity.[14]

Gregory Dix, again, has made an important suggestion in the matter of baptism. He believes on historical grounds that baptism and confirmation were originally part of one rite. To this day the Orthodox churches give infants the communion immediately after baptism. Dix certainly does not propose this; but he does show that baptism and confirmation could be interpreted as two aspects of one sacramental action of the Church. Infant baptism then should never be regarded as "normal." The completion of baptism, and therefore its real significance as a means of grace, would depend upon confirmation which requires a free personal decision.[15]

On the Protestant side Karl Barth has come out against infant baptism, a radical move for a theologian of the Reformed Church.[16] Oscar Cullmann and T. W. Manson have argued against Barth's conclusion on Biblical and theological grounds.[17] It is doubtful if the matter can be settled on the basis of what the first Christians did. There seems no indisputable answer there. And in any case, as Manson says, we should still have to face the issues ourselves. The real question is how baptism should be interpreted within our understanding of God's redemptive action. That the child who is born into a Christian home and presented before the Church as a participant in its life stands in a special relation to the redemptive processes, cannot be denied. But it is surely upon the faith of the community and the later faith, as may be, of the one baptized that the positive action of God's grace depends. The fact of having undergone a particular ceremony surely does not change the personal relationship to God of a child who does not even know what is going on; but it may affect parents and congregation and thus open up new possibilities for the future.

Another move toward modification from within the Anglo-Catholic group comes in connection with one of the most difficult points of all, the claim that the episcopate is necessary to the Church. Some signs indicate that the Anglo-Catholic attitude here has hardened rather changed. The book edited by Bishop K. E. Kirk, *The Apostolic Ministry,* laid down the doctrine that the episcopate as the continuation of the apostolic ministry is the one essential ministry in the Church, and that all other ministry is dependent upon it. But the publication of this thesis brought forth a considerable protest first of all from other Anglicans. Bishops Stephen Neill and A. E. J. Rawlinson have criticized it vigorously, partly on the ground that there is no basis for the claim that the historic Church has never departed from this tradition.[18] The Protestant T. W. Manson has stated a counterthesis that the only essential ministry in the Church is Christ's and all other ministries are dependent upon that.[19]

A hopeful consequence of this discussion is that there are moves from within the Anglo-Catholic group toward rethinking the nature of the episcopate. Significantly enough, this rethinking is reflected in *The Apostolic Ministry* itself. Bishop Kirk admits in his introduction that not all the contributors to that volume hold identical views of the present form of the episcopate. Some hesitate to offer to other churches an office which has taken on such large administrative functions that its spiritual significance is obscured. Father Hebert and the present Archbishop of Canterbury have called for a reconception of the bishop's office to enhance its spiritual stature and leadership.[20]

Many free churchmen have been willing to admit the necessity of the episcopal function; but they have held that this function, authority and unifying leadership has been exercised in the Church through other offices than that of the bishop. Presbyterians speak of the "corporate episcopate" through the presbyteries which confer ministerial standing.[21] Some Congregationalists are awakening to the full dimensions of the questions about episcopacy in relation to the unity of the Church. British Congregational theologians have proposed the development of explicit Congregational forms of episcopacy.[22] In 1957 a joint report on relations between Anglican and Presbyterian churches suggested the reconsideration of aspects of episcopacy in Anglicanism and also suggested the consideration by Presbyterian churches of the acceptance of the ministry of bishops. The first reception given the latter suggestion in the Scottish General Assembly indicated that any immediate prospect for such a move was quite dim. Still, it is clear that episcopal churches are reconsidering the meaning of episcopacy, and non-episcopal churches are asking themselves where their present orders may fall short in presenting the fullness of the one universal community of faith.[23]

These matters of liturgy and church order are not peripheral to the central concerns of Christianity. Liturgy is the language in which the Church continually gives form to its prayer and its confession of faith. Church order is the social structure provided for the new personal relationships created in Jesus Christ. Both liturgy and order are valid in the measure that they serve the work of the Holy Spirit.

IV

As we close this review of the movement toward "internal ecumenicity" it will be well to note that at the Ecumenical Faith and Order Conference in Lund, Sweden, in 1952, a significant development took place in the general discussion of the nature of the Church. It was recognized at Lund that there is no way to a deeper meeting across the traditions which divide the churches apart from a re-examination of the ultimate criteria which apply to all judgments concerning doctrine, polity, and worship. Specifically, the churches must consider again the revelation in Christ as the foundation of all that the Church is. How does each communion grasp and interpret Christ's lordship over the Church? Unless we can discuss that fundamental issue, we cannot really get at the Christian basis for church life.

This insight was reinforced at Lund by the introduction into the discussion of some analysis of so-called "non-theological factors" which historically have divided and shaped the churches. This involved a consideration of political and cultural factors which have affected the many traditions and their practices, and have made it difficult to achieve mutual understanding. We look at one another through the distorting glasses created by centuries of conflict, social division, and institutional habit.

The recognition that there are such factors can lead to a re-appraisal of historic differences. It was quickly pointed out at Lund that there really are no "non-theological" factors in church life, for everything may finally be understood in relation to the faith of the Church; but it should be possible to make clear that in the ultimate criterion of Christian faith, the Word of God in Christ, there is a judgment upon all traditions. In planning for ecumenical study after Lund, commissions have been established throughout the Church to deal with the three themes of Christ and the Church, Tradition, and Worship. As the commissions have started to work there appears to be a new attempt to interpret the fundamental source of all church life in the Christian message, and it may be that some new perspectives in ecumenical theology will appear.[24]

V

In this chapter we could give only a few illustrations of the theological self-criticism which is breaking through to new forms of church life today. The picture could be enlarged by considering similar movements in the Orthodox churches, and the younger churches of Asia like that of South India. There are also important movements in Jewish theology which show that a basic discussion between Christianity and Judaism at a new level of understanding and profound searching is now possible.

But these must be left for other books. We are reminded that the true Church is not only greater than any one of the organized churches, but is greater than all of them. Wherever, according to their lights, men acknowledge God's holy love and begin to respond to it, there is the Church, either in being or in preparation. The caution appropriate at the end of our discussion is that the boundaries of the true Church are known only to God.

Simone Weil, the French writer whose works of penetrating genius are just beginning to be available in English, saw through to the ultimate freedom of God's grace above all human forms. Miss Weil was a Jewess who lived in the most intimate and searching conversation with Christian thought, especially Roman Catholicism. She distrusted the strong emphasis on the Church as the Mystical Body of Christ. She feared it reflected within a sacred society something of the desperate search for the security of "belonging" which was so perversely exploited by Nazism. In her words:

> Social enthusiasms have such power today, they raise people so effectively to the supreme degree of heroism in suffering and death, that I think it is as well that a few sheep should remain outside the fold in order to bear witness that the love of Christ is essentially something different.[25]

This is surely an authentic Christian word. The Church which remains most profoundly aware of its own humanity is closer to the Kingdom of God than the one which is so confident of its heritage of grace that it forgets God can raise up "children of Abraham" from the very stones.

EPILOGUE

THEOLOGIANS are an embattled company, partly among themselves, but mostly with those who look with suspicion on what
comes out of theological discussions. Churchmen suspect theologians
of suffocating the life of faith under a blanket of technical verbiage.
Outside the Church, and inside too, theology is suspected of being
an archaic way of thinking which blocks scientific progress by its
dependence upon a mysteriously revealed source of knowledge
rather than upon the tests of reason and experience.

These charges are undoubtedly true for some theologians all of
the time and for all of them some of the time. There are occupa-
tional hazards and diseases in this way of serving the Christian
faith, and some of them afflict the soul itself. But I hope that something of the true spirit of those who engage in theological labor
and believe in it has become visible in our study of present-day
problems. What theologians are doing is as necessary to human
life as breathing. Man is the being who asks for the meaning of his
own existence. He must know who he is and who God is, what
justice is, what to hope for. All the powerful movements in the
world today offer men something more than bread. They offer
faith and a way of life.

Now giving answers to ultimate questions is not the restricted
privilege of a few professional theologians. Everyone who tries
to say what the Christian faith and life is for him, is engaging in
theological work. The important matter is to say what it is that

makes Christian thinking different from other ways of thinking. It is close to science, to philosophy, and in a way to art, yet not identical with any of these.

The key to the distinctive nature of theology is found in its own proper source, the reality we call Jesus Christ. Christians think about the meaning of life not on the basis of abstract ideas alone, nor on the basis of experience in general; but from the standpoint of this one strand of history where we believe life is so broken open for us that we can see into its depth more than we can anywhere else. We never exhaust the meaning of Jesus Christ. All human knowledge is relevant to our knowledge of him. He does not destroy but fulfills all other truth, else he would not be the Christ. But since this source of our faith is found in a personal history, and in a living community of persons, we have always to acknowledge a certain limitation on our intellectual formulations of the faith. Theological doctrines are valid only in so far as they point us to the fuller truth which is there in God's word in Christ. The intellectualism of theology is qualified by faith. This ought to lead the Christian thinker to a respect for all honest searching for truth, and a humility with regard to his own formulas.

Theology which thus has its source and norm in a personal reality requires a personal decision on the part of the theologian. He thinks within a community of faith, and he must know what it is to risk his intellectual enterprise and his life on commitments to the God we know in Christ. Theological thinking can be objective, but it cannot be detached from personal decision. It is just here that theology is able to speak most directly to the need of man today. For our problem is to realize a human community where men can think and live with one another as persons and not as things.

Man has incredible power in his hands. Scientific knowledge can build or destroy; it can heal or kill. But science by itself cannot determine how knowledge will be used. Only man can determine that, and the question is by what spirit and for what ends will his choices be made. The Christian faith is that we are created for a personal life in a community where each is sustained by the others. We can have this life only if in humility we confess our dependence upon the Holy Source of Life, acknowledge God's judgment on human idols and confess our own continuing temptation to idolatry. Christianity believes in man more deeply than any other historic faith; because it believes that man's spirit can be opened to the cleansing and humbling which comes when God meets him in self-giving love. The Christian faith gives no pat answers or panaceas. What it says is that life in all its struggle is good at the core, and that under God there is offered new life in the love which fills all struggle with meaning. It is not, therefore, tradition which keeps theological thinking alive. It is our persistent human need to find a satisfying personal existence which keeps the tradition relevant for every age. Theological work has its peculiar difficulties, but it is sustained by the hope which comes from Him in whom all truth coheres.

NOTES

Chapter I. *The Theological Renaissance*

1 Alan Richardson, *Christian Apologetics* (New York: Harper & Brothers, 1947), p. 83.
2 Norberto Bobbio, *The Philosophy of Decadentism* (New York: Macmillan, 1948), pp. 44-45.
3 Paul Tillich, "The Present Theological Situation," in *Theology Today*, Vol. VI, No. 3, 1949, p. 303.
4 Editorial in *Life* magazine, Dec. 24, 1951, p. 20.
5 Karl Löwith, *Meaning in History* (Chicago: University of Chicago Press, 1949), p. 4.
6 Arnold Toynbee, *A Study of History* (New York: Oxford University Press, 1947). Two-volume abridgment.
7 Herbert Butterfield, *Christianity and History* (New York: Charles Scribner's Sons, 1950), p. 107.
8 M. Heidegger, *Existence and Being,* ed. by W. Brock (Chicago: Henry Regnery, 1949).
9 Bertrand Russell, *A History of Western Philosophy* (New York: Simon & Schuster, 1945), p. 834.
10 Gilbert Ryle, A. J. Ayer, *et al., The Revolution in Philosophy* (talks on the B.B.C., 1956).
11 G. C. Stead, "How Theologians Reason," in *Faith and Logic,* ed. by Basil Mitchell (London: Allen & Unwin, 1957), p. 108.
12 John Wisdom, "Gods," in *Philosophy and Psycho-Analysis* (New York: Philosophical Library, 1953).
13 R. M. Hare in *New Essays in Philosophical Theology,* ed. by A. Flew and A. MacIntyre (New York: Macmillan, 1955).
14 John Hick, *Faith and Knowledge* (Ithaca: Cornell University Press, 1957).
15 Austin Farrer, "A Starting-Point for the Examination of Theological Belief," in *Faith and Logic.*
16 Ernst Cassirer, *Language and Myth* (New York: Harper & Brothers, 1946).
17 Susanne K. Langer, *Philosophy in a New Key* (Cambridge: Harvard University Press, 1942), p. 149.

18 Thomas Torrance, *Calvin's Doctrine of Man* (London: Lutterworth, 1949).

Chapter II. *The Bible and Christian Truth*

1 Rom. 1:19 (Moffatt).
2 Emil Brunner, *Man in Revolt* (New York: Charles Scribner's Sons, 1939), p. 65; cf. pp. 241 ff.
3 Martin Luther, *Tischreden,* quoted in Robert M. Grant, *The Bible in the Church* (New York: Macmillan, 1948), p. 114.
4 Karl Barth, *The Doctrine of the Word of God* (Edinburgh: T. & T. Clark, 1936), p. 302.
5 Karl Barth, *Dogmatics in Outline* (New York: Philosophical Library, 1949), p. 59.
6 *Ibid.,* p. 26.
7 Emil Brunner, "The New Barth," in *The Scottish Journal of Theology,* June, 1951.
8 David Cairns, *The Image of God in Man* (New York: Philosophical Library, 1953), p. 194.
9 Karl Barth, *Christ and Adam* (New York: Harper & Brothers, 1956), pp. 31 ff. Cf. Introduction by Wilhelm Pauck.
10 Emil Brunner, *The Divine-Human Encounter* (Philadelphia: Westminster Press, 1943).
11 Rudolph Bultmann, "New Testament and Mythology," in H.-W. Bartsch, ed., *Kerygma and Myth* (London: S.P.C.K., 1953). Several volumes under the general title *Kerygma und Mythos* continue the critical discussion.
12 John Macquarrie, *An Existentialist Theology* (New York: Macmillan, 1935); Ian Henderson, *Myth in the New Testament* (Chicago: Henry Regnery, 1952); Friedrich Gogarten, *Demythologizing and History* (New York: Charles Scribner's Sons, 1955) are important essays on the problem raised by Bultmann.
13 Karl Barth, *Die Kirchliche Dogmatik* (Munchen: C. Kaiser, 1932-55). Some volumes are published by Zollikon, Zurich. All of volume I (2 parts) and volume IV, part I and II, have been translated into English at present writing.
On the issue raised by Bultmann, see Barth, K.D., III, 2. Rudolph Bultmann, *Essays* (New York: Macmillan, 1955), pp. 259 ff.
14 Volume V of *Kerygma und Mythos,* esp. "Sola Fide" by Adolf Kolping.
15 Paul Tillich, "The Present Theological Situation," *loc. cit.,* p. 305.
16 Paul Tillich, *Systematic Theology,* Vol. I (Chicago: University of Chicago Press, 1951), p. 48. Vol. II (1957).
17 *Ibid.,* Vol. I, p. 49.
18 Walt Whitman, *Democratic Vistas* (Viking Library), pp. 458, 462.
19 Henry Nelson Wieman, *The Source of Human Good* (Chicago: University of Chicago Press, 1946). Cf. H. N. Wieman, *Man's Ultimate*

Commitment (Carbondale: Southern Illinois University Press, 1958).

20 Nels F. S. Ferré, *The Christian Understanding of God* (New York: Harper & Brothers, 1951); *Christ and the Christian* (New York: Harper & Brothers, 1958).

21 Alan Richardson, *Christian Apologetics,* p. 77.

22 Gabriel Marcel, "Theism and Personal Relationships," *Cross Currents,* Fall, 1950, p. 42.

23 Hunter Guthrie, *Introduction au Probleme de L'Histoire de la Philosophie* (Paris: Alcan, 1937), p. 270, translation mine.

24 Robert Barrat, "Reaction to the Encyclical," *The Commonweal,* Oct. 6, 1950, pp. 628-30.

25 William Temple, *Nature, Man and God* (New York: Macmillan, 1935), pp. 316-21.

26 Austin Farrer, *The Glass of Vision* (Westminster: Dacre Press, 1948).

27 David Roberts, *Psychotherapy and a Christian View of Man* (New York: Charles Scribner's Sons, 1950), p. 133.

Chapter III. *God and the World*

1 John A. T. Robinson, *Honest to God* (London: SCM Press, 1963) Cf. David L. Edwards, ed. *The Honest to God Debate* (Philadelphia: The Westminster Press, 1963).

2 Dietrich Bonhoeffer, *Prisoner for God: Letters and Papers from Prison,* tr. by Reginald Fuller (New York: Macmillan, 1953). See an excellent volume of studies of Bonhoeffer edited by Martin E. Marty, *The Place of Bonhoeffer* (New York: Association Press, 1962).

3 Dietrich Bonhoeffer, *The Communion of Saints,* tr. by R. Gregor Smith (New York: Harper and Row, 1960), pp. 111-112.

4 Cf. Gerhard Ebeling, *The Nature of Faith,* Engl. tr. (Philadelphia: Muhlenberg Press, 1961), pp. 182-191.

5 Dietrich Bonhoeffer, *Letters from Prison,* pp. 190-191.

6 *Ibid.* p. 220.

7 For relevant discussion of the new ethical challenge in the world situation see *Christian Social Ethics in a Changing World,* edited by John C. Bennett (New York: Association Press, 1966).

8 Robert W. Spike, *The Freedom Revolution and the Churches* (New York: Association Press, 1965), p. 83.

9 Friedrich Nietzsche, *Thus Spake Zarathustra,* IV, 16-17.

10 Søren Kierkegaard, *Concluding Unscientific Postscript* (Princeton University Press, 1941), p. 219.

11 Martin Buber, *The Eclipse of God* (New York: Harper & Row, 1957).

12 William Hamilton, "The Death of God Theology," *The Christian Scholar,* Vol. XLVII, No. 1, Spring, 1965, p. 45.

13 William Hamilton, "The Shape of a Radical Theology," *The Christian Century,* Vol. LXXII, No. 6, Oct. 6, 1965.

14 Thomas J. J. Altizer, *Mircea Eliade and the Dialectic of the Sacred* (Philadelphia: Westminster Press, 1963), and "Creative Negation in Theology," *The Christian Century,* Vol. LXXXII, No. 27, July 7, 1965.

15 Paul Van Buren, *The Secular Meaning of the Gospel* (New York: Macmillan, 1963). See pp. 101 ff. and p. 156.

16 See for example A. J. Ayer's Oxford Inaugural Lecture, *Philosophy and Language* (Oxford: Clarendon Press, 1960). On Wieman's theology see *The Empirical Theology of Henry Nelson Wieman,* ed. by Robert Bretall (New York: Macmillan, 1963).

17 Langdon Gilkey, "Is God Dead" and "God is Not Dead," in *The Voice, The Crozier Quarterly.*

18 Helmut Gollwitzer, *The Existence of God as Confessed by Faith* (Philadelphia: The Westminster Press, 1965), p. 130.

19 *Ibid.* pp. 131–132.

20 *Ibid.* p. 149.

21 Ernst Fuchs, *Studies of the Historical Jesus* (London: SCM Press, 1964), pp. 425–427.

22 James M. Robinson, *A New Quest of the Historical Jesus* (Naperville, Ill.: Allenson, 1959).

23 *Ibid.* pp. 68–69. The quotation is from Gerhard Ebeling, *Theologie und Verkündigung,* p. 14 f.

24 A. N. Whitehead, *Process and Reality* (New York, Macmillan, 1929), p. 17.

25 The first quotation is from Gerhard Ebeling, *Word and Faith* (Philadelphia: Fortress Press, 1963), p. 214.
The last two quotations are from Ebeling, *The Nature of Faith* (Philadelphia: Muhlenberg Press, 1961), p. 21, p. 62.

26 Ian Ramsey, *Religious Language* (London: SCM Press, 1957). Cf. *Christian Discourse, some Logical explorations* (New York: Oxford University Press, 1965).

27 Claude Tresmontant, *A Study of Hebrew Thought,* Eng. tr. (New York: Desclée Co. 1960).

28 Peter Schoonenberg, *God's World in the Making* (Pittsburgh: Duquesne University Press, 1964), p. 179.

Chapter IV. *Christian Ethics and Society*

1 *Amsterdam Assembly of the World Council of Churches,* report of section III (1948).

2 *The Responsible Society in a World Perspective* (New York: Harper & Brothers, 1954), p. 78.

3 Edward Duff, S.J., *The Social Thought of the World Council of Churches* (New York: Association Press, 1956).

4 Barbara Ward, *Faith and Freedom; a Study of Western Society* (London: H. Hamilton, 1954).

5 Jacques Maritain, *The Rights of Man and Natural Law* (New York: Charles Scribner's Sons, 1943), pp. 112-13.

6 John Courtney Murray, "Contemporary Orientations of Catholic Thought on Church and State in the Light of History," in *Cross-Currents,* Fall, 1951.

7 Jacques Maritain, *op. cit.,* p. 24.

8 W. A. Visser 't Hooft, *The Kingship of Christ* (New York: Harper & Brothers, 1948).

9 Karl H. Hertz, *Bible Commonwealth and Holy Experiment,* unpublished dissertation, University of Chicago, 1948.

10 Henry Nelson Wieman, *The Directive in History* (Boston: Beacon Press, 1949), chap. 3.

11 Anders Nygren, *Agape and Eros,* revised English translation by Philip S. Watson (London: S.P.C.K., 1953).

12 Reinhold Niebuhr, *The Nature and Destiny of Man,* Vol. II (New York: Charles Scribner's Sons, 1943), chap. 3.

13 Emil Brunner, *Justice and the Social Order* (New York: Harper & Brothers, 1945).

14 Paul Ramsey, *Basic Christian Ethics* (New York: Charles Scribner's Sons, 1950), pp. 100-101.

15 *Ibid.,* p. 14.

16 *Ibid.,* p. 242.

17 *Ibid.,* p. 358.

18 Reinhold Niebuhr, *The Children of Light and the Children of Darkness* (New York: Charles Scribner's Sons, 1944), p. xi.

19 Ramsey, *op. cit.,* p. 344.

20 Cf. Gregory Vlastos and R. B. Y. Scott, *Towards the Christian Revolution* (Chicago: Willett Clark, 1936), chap. 3; John MacMurray, *Reason and Emotion* (New York: Appleton-Century-Crofts, 1936); H. N. Wieman, *The Source of Human Good* (Chicago: University of Chicago Press, 1946).

21 Harvey Cox, *The Secular City* (New York: Macmillan, 1965), p. 81.

22 *Ibid.* pp. 261, 265.

23 H. Richard Niebuhr, *The Responsible Self* (New York: Harper & Row, 1963). Cf. his *Radical Monotheism and Western Culture* (New York: Harper & Row, 1960), esp. pp. 100 ff.

24 Paul Lehmann, *Ethics in a Christian Context* (New York: Harper and Row, 1963), pp. 353, 366.

25 *Ibid.* p. 131.

26 *Ibid.* p. 386.

27 *Ibid.* p. 129.

28 William K. Frankena, *Ethics* (New Jersey: Prentice Hall, 1963).

29 Paul Ramsey, *Deeds and Rules in Christian Ethics, Scottish Journal of Theology,* occasional papers, No. 11.

30 *Ibid.* pp. 85-89.

31 Paul Ramsey, *The Limits of Nuclear War,* published by the Council on Religion and International Affairs, 1963. *Christian Ethics and the Sit-In* (New York: Association Press, 1961).

32 Joseph Fletcher and Herbert McCabe, "The New Morality," *Commonweal*, Vol. LXXXIII, No. 14, 1966. Cf. Karl Rahner, *Gefahren im Heutigen Katholizimus* (Johannes Verlag, Einsiedeln, 1950), on the dangers of a situations ethic.

33 H. Richard Niebuhr, *Christ and Culture* (New York: Harper & Row, 1951).

34 Jacques Ellul, "Propositions Concerning the Christian Attitude Toward Law," *Oklahoma Law Review*, Vol. 12, 134, 1959, p. 142.

35 *Ibid.* p. 141.

36 Jacques Ellul, "Law as Representation of Value," *Natural Law Forum*, 10:54, 1965.

37 William Stringfellow, "The Christian Lawyer as a Churchman," in *Christian Faith and Human Law*, a symposium in *The Christian Scholar*, Vol. XL, No. 3, Sept. 1957, p. 235.

38 Edmond Cahn, *The Sense of Injustice* (Bloomington, Indiana University Press, 1949, 1964).
The Moral Decision (Bloomington: Indiana University Press, 1955).

39 Glanville Williams, *The Sanctity of Life and the Criminal Law* (London: Faber and Faber, 1958).

40 Joseph Fletcher, *Morals and Medicine* (Princeton: Princeton University Press, 1954); see symposium on Fletcher's book in *New York University Law Review*, Vol. 31, No. 7, 1956.

Chapter V. *Jesus Christ in History and Faith*

1 Donald Baillie, *God Was in Christ* (New York: Charles Scribner's Sons, 1948), p. 65.

2 Reinhold Niebuhr, *The Nature and Destiny of Man* (New York: Charles Scribner's Sons, 1943), Vol. II, chap. 2.

3 John Knox, *Christ the Lord* (New York: Harper & Brothers, 1945), *passim*.

4 *Ibid.*, p. 73.

5 Baillie, *op. cit.*, p. 47.

6 Allan D. Galloway, *The Cosmic Christ* (New York: Harper & Brothers, 1951), pp. 233, 235-36, 239.

7 Quoted Baillie, *op. cit.*, p. 49.

8 Karl Barth, *The Doctrine of the Word of God*, p. 188.

9 Emil Brunner, *The Mediator* (Philadelphia: Westminster Press, 1947), p. 343 n.

10 Rudolph Bultmann, *Theology of the New Testament*, Vol. I (New York: Charles Scribner's Sons, 1951), translated by Kendrick Grobel, pp. 294-95.

11 *Ibid.*, p. 303.

12 *Ibid.*, p. 35.

13 Tillich, *Systematic Theology*, Vol. I, p. 136.

14 *Ibid.*, p. 133.
15 Paul Tillich, *Systematic Theology,* Vol. II, p. 111.
16 *Ibid.*, p. 148.
17 Reinhold Niebuhr, *The Nature and Destiny of Man,* Vol. II, p. 72.
18 Donald Baillie, *op. cit.*, p. 127.
19 *Ibid.*, pp. 93, 117, 129.
20 Martin Luther, quoted in I. A. Dorner, *History of the Doctrine of the Person of Christ* (Edinburgh, 1866), Vol. 4, pp. 93-94 n. Cf. A. Harnack, *History of Dogma* (Boston, 1900), Vol. 7, pp. 198-99.
21 Nels Ferré, *The Christian Understanding of God,* p. 86. Cf. J. K. Mozley, *The Impassibility of God* (Cambridge: Cambridge University Press, 1926).
22 Nicolas Berdyaev, *The Destiny of Man* (London: Centenary Press, 1937), p. 371.
23 For the Draft Statement and comments see *The Christian Century,* April 9, 1952. Cf. Paul Minear, *Christian Hope and the Second Coming* (Philadelphia-Westminster Press, 1954).
24 See "The Christian Hope and the Millennium," a series of articles in *Christianity Today* beginning in Vol. II, No. 24, Sept. 15, 1958.
25 In a lecture at the Chicago Theological Seminary in 1950.
26 E. L. Mascall, *Christ, The Christian, and the Church* (New York: Longman's Green and Co., 1946), p. 65.

Chapter VI. *The Church*

1 Quoted in R. N. Flew and R. E. Davies, eds., *The Catholicity of Protestantism* (London: Lutterworth, 1950), p. 8.
2 *Ibid.*, p. 27.
3 R. N. Flew, *Jesus and His Church* (Nashville: Abingdon Press, 1938), p. 179.
4 Karl Schmidt, *The Church* (London: Adam and Charles Black, 1950), translated from Kittel's *Worterbuch zum neuen Testament.*
5 Paul Tillich, *The Protestant Era* (Chicago: University of Chicago Press, 1948), especially chaps. 11, 14.
6 Yngve Brilioth, *Eucharistic Faith and Practice. Evangelical and Catholic* (London: S.P.C.K., 1930), p. viii.
7 Two recent Protestant studies are Elmer Freeman *The Lord's Supper in Protestantism* (New York: Macmillan, 1945), and Harold Fey, *The Lord's Supper: Seven Meanings* (New York: Harper & Brothers, 1948).
8 William Temple, *The Genius of the Church of England,* quoted in A. E. Baker, *William Temple's Teaching* (Philadelphia: Westminster Press, 1951), p. 103.
9 I am much indebted here to the doctoral dissertation of Ernest B. Koenker in the library of the University of Chicago, *The Liturgical Movement in the Roman Catholic Church* (1950). Cf. Romano Guardini, *The Spirit of the Liturgy* (London: Sheed and Ward, 1937).

10 Text and commentary in *The Clergy Monthly,* Vol. 27, No. 9.

11 Hans Küng, "What Has the Council Done?" *Commonweal,* Vol. lxxxiii, No. 15, Jan. 21, 1966, p. 466.

12 Frederick W. Dillistone, *The Structure of the Divine Society* (Philadelphia: Westminster Press, 1951), p. 221.

13 Dom Gregory Dix, *The Shape of the Liturgy* (Westminster: Dacre Press, 1945), p. 696.

14 *The Theology of Christian Initiation,* report of a commission appointed by the Archbishops of Canterbury and York.

15 Dom Gregory Dix, *The Theology of Confirmation in Relation to Baptism* (Westminster, 1946).

16 Karl Barth, *The Teaching of the Church Regarding Baptism* (London: Student Christian Movement Press, 1948).

17 Oscar Cullmann, *Baptism in the New Testament* (Chicago: Henry Regnery, 1950). T. W. Manson, lectures on baptism at McCormick Theological Seminary, Chicago, 1952.

18 Stephen Neill and others, *The Ministry of the Church* (London: Canterbury Press, 1947); A. E. J. Rawlinson, *Problems of Re-union* (London: Eyre and Spottiswoode, 1952).

19 T. W. Manson, *The Church's Ministry* (Philadelphia: Westminster Press, 1948).

20 K. E. Kirk, *The Apostolic Ministry* (London: Hodder and Stoughton, 1946), reissued with new foreword by A. Farrer, 1957, pp. 48, 532-33.

21 T. F. Torrance, review of Rawlinson, *op. cit.,* in *The Scottish Journal of Theology,* Dec., 1951, p. 430.

22 Nathaniel Micklem, *Congregationalism and Episcopacy* (London: Independent Press).

23 *Joint Report on Relations Between Anglican and Presbyterian Churches* (London: S.P.C.K., 1957).

24 *Report of the Third World Conference on Faith and Order, Lund, Sweden,* 1952. Faith and Order Papers, No. 15. Cf. No. 10, *Social and Cultural Factors in Church Divisions.*

SUPPLEMENTARY BOOK LIST
Titles discussed but not quoted in the text

Aulén, Gustaf, *Church, Law, and Society* (New York: Charles Scribner's Sons, 1948).

———, *The Faith of the Christian Church* (Philadelphia: Muhlenberg Press, 1948).

Ayer, A. J., *Language, Truth and Logic* (New York: Dover Publications, 1946).

Baillie, John, *Our Knowledge of God* (New York: Charles Scribner's Sons, 1939).

Barth, Karl, *The Humanity of God* (Richmond, Virginia: John Knox Press, 1960).

———, *The Letter to the Romans* (Trans. of 6th Ed. London: Oxford University Press, 1933).

Bennett, John C., *Christian Realism* (New York: Charles Scribner's Sons, 1941).

———, *Christian Ethics and Social Policy* (New York: Charles Scribner's Sons, 1946).

———, *Christians and the State* (New York: Charles Scribner's Sons, 1958).

Berdyaev, Nicolas, *Slavery and Freedom* (New York: Charles Scribner's Sons, 1944).

Bergendoff, Conrad, *Christ as Authority* (Rock Island: Augustana Book Concern, 1947).

Bonhoeffer, Dietrich, *Act and Being* (New York: Harper & Row, 1961).

———, *Ethics,* ed. by Eberhard Bethge (New York: Macmillan, 1955, 1965).

Bonthius, Robert, *Christian Paths to Self-Acceptance* (New York: King's Crown Press, 1948).

Bouquet, A. C., *The Christian Faith and Non-Christian Religions* (New York: Harper & Brothers, 1959).

Brunner, Emil, *Dogmatics,* Vol. I-II (Philadelphia: Westminster Press, 1940-52).

Buber, Martin, *I and Thou* (Edinburgh: T. & T. Clark, 1937).

Burrows, Millar, *The Dead Sea Scrolls* (New York: Viking Press, 1955).

———, *More Light on the Dead Sea Scrolls* (New York: Viking Press, 1958).

Cahn, Edmond, *The Moral Decision* (Bloomington: Indiana University Press, 1955).

———, *The Sense of Injustice* (New York: New York University Press, 1949).

Camus, Albert, *The Fall* (New York: Alfred A. Knopf, 1956).

Carlson, Edgar, *The Reinterpretation of Luther* (Philadelphia: Westminster Press, 1948).

Cobb, John B. Jr., *A Christian Natural Theology* (Philadelphia: Westminster Press, 1965).

Cross, Frank, *The Ancient Library of Qumran* (London: Duckworth, 1958).

Cullmann, Oscar, *Christ and Time* (Philadelphia: Westminster Press, 1940).

D'Arcy, M. C., *The Mind and Heart of Love* (New York: Henry Holt, 1947).

DeWolf, L. Harold, *A Theology of the Living Church* (New York: Harper & Brothers, 1953).

Farmer, H. H., *Revelation and Religion* (New York: Harper & Brothers, 1954).

Flew, A. and MacIntyre, A., eds., *New Essays in Philosophical Theology* (New York: Macmillan, 1955).

Frankel, Charles, *The Case for Modern Man* (New York: Harper & Brothers, 1956).

Grant, Robert M., *The Secret Sayings of Jesus* in collaboration with David Noel Freedman (Garden City, N. Y.: Doubleday, 1960).

Hamilton, William, *The New Essence of Christianity* (New York: Association Press, 1961).

Hartshorne, Charles, *The Divine Relativity* (New Haven: Yale University Press, 1948).

———, *Man's Vision of God* (New York: Harper & Brothers, 1941).

Hazelton, Roger, *Renewing the Mind* (New York: Macmillan, 1949).

Hebert, A. G., *The Form of the Church* (London: Faber and Faber, 1954).

———, *The Throne of David* (New York: Morehouse-Gorham, 1941).

Heim, Karl, *The Transformation of the Scientific World View* (New York: Harper & Brothers, 1953).

Hocking, William Ernest, *Religions and a World Faith* (New York: Macmillan, 1940).

———, *The Coming World Civilization* (New York: Harper & Brothers, 1956).

Huxley, Julian, *Religion without Revelation* (New York: Harper & Brothers, 1957).

Jung, C. G., *Answer to Job* (London: Routledge & Kegan Paul, 1954).

Kraemer, Hendrick, *The Christian Message in a Non-Christian World* (New York: Harper & Brothers, 1938).

———, *Religion and the Christian Faith* (Philadelphia: Westminster Press, 1956).

Lefever, Ernest, *Ethics and United States Foreign Policy* (New York: Meridian Books, 1957).

Loomer, Bernard M., "Christian Faith and Process Philosophy," in *The Journal of Religion*, Vol. 29, No. 3, 1949.

Lortz, J., *Reformation in Deutschland* (Freiburg: 1947).

McGill, Arthur C. *The Celebration of Flesh* (New York: Association Press, 1964).

Meland, Bernard E., *Faith and Culture* (New York: Oxford University Press, 1953).

————, *The Re-Awakening of Christian Faith* (New York: Macmillan, 1949).

Miegge, Giovanni, *The Virgin Mary* (London: Lutterworth, 1956).

Minear, Paul, *The Kingdom and the Power* (Philadelphia: Westminster Press, 1950).

Niebuhr, H. Richard, Pauck, Wilhelm, Miller, Francis P., *The Church Against the World* (Chicago: Willett Clark, 1935).

Niebuhr, H. Richard, *The Meaning of Revelation* (New York: Macmillan, 1941).

————, *Christ and Culture* (New York: Harper & Brothers, 1951).

Niebuhr, Reinhold, *Faith and History* (New York: Charles Scribner's Sons, 1949).

————, *The Irony of American History* (New York: Charles Scribner's Sons, 1952).

————, *The Children of Light and the Children of Darkness* (New York: Charles Scribner's Sons, 1945).

————, *Moral Man and Immoral Society* (New York: Charles Scribner's Sons, 1932).

Niebuhr, Richard Reinhold, *Resurrection and Historical Reason* (New York: Charles Scribner's Sons, 1957).

Nichols, James Hastings, *Democracy and the Churches* (Philadelphia: Westminster Press, 1951).

Parker, T. H. L., ed., *Essays in Christology for Karl Barth* (London: Lutterworth, 1956).

Pauck, Wilhelm, *The Heritage of the Reformation* (Boston: Beacon Press, 1950).

Pittenger, W. Norman, *Christ and the Christian Faith* (New York: Round Table Press, 1941).

Ramsdell, Edward, *The Christian Perspective* (Nashville: Abingdon Press, 1950).

Ramsey, Paul, ed., *Faith and Ethics: The Theology of H. Richard Niebuhr* (Harper & Brothers, 1957).

Ramsey, A. Michael, *The Gospel and the Catholic Church* (London: Longmans Green, 1956).

Reid, J. K. S., *The Authority of Scripture* (New York: Harper & Brothers, 1957).

Ross, Floyd, *Addressed to Christians: Isolationism vs. World Community* (New York: Harper & Brothers, 1950).

Rupp, Gordon, *The Righteousness of God* (London: Hodder & Stoughton, 1953).

Scott, Nathan A. Jr., ed. *The Tragic Vision and the Christian Faith* (New York: Association Press, 1957).

Smith, Wilfred Cantwell, *The Meaning and End of Religion* (New York: Macmillan, 1962).

Stendahl, Krister, ed., *The Scrolls and the New Testament* (New York: Harper & Brothers, 1957).

Stokes, Anson Phelps, *Church and State in the United States* (New York: Harper & Brothers, 1950).

Teilhard de Chardin, Pierre, *The Phenomenon of Man* (New York: Harper & Row, 1959).

——, *The Divine Milieu* (New York: Harper & Row, 1960).

Temple, William, *Christianity and Social Order* (London: S.C.M. Press, 1950).

Thornton, L. S., *The Incarnate Lord* (London: Longmans Green, 1928).

Toynbee, Arnold, *Christianity among the Religions of the World* (New York: Charles Scribner's Sons, 1957).

Vahanian, Gabriel, *The Death of God* (New York: G. Braziller, 1961).

Watson, Philip, *Let God Be God* (Philadelphia: Muhlenburg Press, 1949).

Weizäcker, C. F. von, *The History of Nature* (University of Chicago Press, 1949).

West, Charles, *Communism and the Theologians* (London: S.C.M. Press, 1958).

Wilder, Amos, *Modern Poetry and the Christian Tradition* (New York: Chas. Scribner's Sons, 1952).

Williams, Daniel D., *God's Grace and Man's Hope* (New York: Harper & Brothers, 1949).

Wilson, Edmund, *A Piece of My Mind* (New York: Doubleday, 1958).

Wingren, Gustaf, *Luther on Vocation* (Edinburgh: Oliver & Boyd, 1958; Philadelphia: Muhlenburg, 1957).

Zuurdeeg, Willem, *An Analytical Philosophy of Religion* (Nashville: Abingdon Press, 1958).

INDEX